Aeri's Korean Cookbook 1

Aeri Lee

Thank you for purchasing this book and supporting Aeri's Kitchen. If you would like to see more details about these recipes, including videos, please visit aeriskitchen.com. Be sure to check out all the other recipes while you are there.

This book would not have been possible without the supporters of Aeri's Kitchen. First off, thanks go to the grace of God, and all of the things He has done. Many thanks go out to my family who always support me. My wonderful husband did all the hard work editing, designing and creating this cookbook. Thank you very much. Without his help, I cannot imagine publishing my own cookbook. Thanks also go out to all my fans and subscribers who have been supportive both morally and financially. Sempio has also been very gracious in their support. Amazon created a fantastic self-publishing system that enabled this book to be printed. Google created an advertisement system that allowed partial compensation for all of Aeri's hard work. We hope that this book will become a good gift for our children, who will be able cook and eat mommy's food anytime in the future. God bless you all.

ISBN-13: 978-1475290615
ISBN-10: 1475290616

Aeri's Kitchen is a trademark of Konglishville, Inc.

Appetizers & Snacks

10 Chicken & Veggie Naengchae	7 AeHoBakJeon	15 간장 닭꼬치
15 Chicken Ggochi	16 ConSaelReoDeu	6 감자전
12 Crabstick Jeon	10 DakGaSeumSal GyeoJaNaengChae	11 과일 샐러드
17 Crown Daisy Jeon	6 GamJaJeon	8 궁중 떡볶이
11 Korean Style Fruit Salad	15 GanJang DakGgoChi	10 닭가슴살 겨자냉채
6 Potato Jeon	8 GungJung TteokBokkI	9 떡볶이
14 Rest Stop Gamja	11 GwaIl SaelReoDeu	12 맛살전
8 Royal Palace Tteokbokki	13 HaeMulPaJeon	17 쑥갓전
13 Seafood & Green Onion Jeon	14 HyuGeSoGamJa	7 애호박전
9 Spicy Tteokbokki	12 MatSalJeon	16 콘샐러드
16 Sweet Corn Salad	17 SsukGatJeon	13 해물파전
7 Zucchini Jeon	9 TteokBokkI	14 휴게소감자

Soups & Stews

25 Army Base Jjigae	25 BuDaeJjiGae	19 고등어조림
30 Beef & Radish Guk	23 ChamChi GimChiJjiGae	28 굴떡국
24 Beef & Sea Mustard Guk	21 DongTaeGuk	21 동태국
22 Extra Soft Tofu Jjigae	20 EoMukGuk	25 부대찌개
20 Fish Cake Guk	19 GoDeungEoJoRim	30 소고기 무국
21 Haddock Guk	28 GulTteokGuk	24 소고기 미역국
27 Mussel Tang	27 HongHabTang	31 수제비
28 Oyster Rice Cake Guk	18 JoGiMaeUnTang	22 순두부찌개
31 Simple Sujaebi	26 KongNaMulGuk	20 어묵국
26 Soybean Sprout Guk	24 SoGoGi MiYeokGuk	29 육개장
29 Spicy Beef & Veggie Guk	30 SoGoGi MuGuk	18 조기매운탕
19 Spicy Mackerel Jorim	31 SuJeBi	23 참치 김치찌개
18 Spicy Yellow Croaker Maeuntang	22 SunDuBuJjiGae	26 콩나물국
23 Tuna Kimchi Jjigae	29 YukGaeJang	27 홍합탕

Sides

42 Baby Potato Jorim	43 AeHoBakBokkEum	38 감자조림
35 Bellflower Root Muchim	42 AlGamJaJoRim	45 깻잎김치
52 Cucumber Chojeolim	36 BuChuGimChi	35 도라지무침
37 Cucumber Kimchi	35 DoRaJiMuChim	47 두부부침
46 Cucumber Naengguk	47 DuBuBuChim	39 두부조림
50 Fish Sausage Buchim	39 DuBuJoRim	51 매운 어묵볶음
36 Garlic Chive Kimchi	38 GamJaJoRim	53 무초절임
53 Korean Radish Chojeolim	45 GgaetIpGimChi	40 미역줄기볶음
33 Mung Bean Sprout Namul	41 JwiPoBokkEum	36 부추김치
45 Perilla Kimchi	51 MaeUn EoMukBokkEum	50 소세지부침
44 Pickled Cucumber Muchim	40 MiYeokJulGiBokkEum	33 숙주나물
38 Potato Jorim	53 MuChoJeolIm	32 시금치나물
41 Seasoned Filefish Bokkeum	52 OIChoJeolIm	48 시금치장떡
40 Seaweed Stem Bokkeum	44 OIJiMuChim	42 알감자조림
34 Shredded Cabbage Muchim	46 OINaengGuk	43 애호박볶음
51 Spicy Fish Cake Bokkeum	37 OISoBakI	34 양배추무침
48 Spinach Jangtteok	49 OJingEo MiNaRiChoMuChim	52 오이초절임
32 Spinach Namul	48 SiGeumChiJangTteok	46 오이냉국
49 Squid & Watercress Chomuchim	32 SiGeumChiNaMul	37 오이소박이
47 Tofu Buchim	50 SoSeJiBuChim	44 오이지무침
39 Tofu Jorim	33 SukJuNaMul	49 오징어 미나리초무침
43 Zucchini Bokkeum	34 YangBaeChuMuChim	41 쥐포볶음

Meat & Seafood

68 Andong Jjimdak	68 AnDong JjimDak	57 고추전
55 Beef Bulgogi	58 DakBokkEumTang	62 골뱅이무침
60 Beef Galbi	54 DakGalBi	65 굴전
56 Beef Meatball Twigim	64 GgaetIp GoGiJeon	64 깻잎 고기전
63 Beef Patty Galbi	57 GoChuJeon	54 닭갈비
67 Beef Short Rib Jjim	62 GolBaengIMuChim	58 닭볶음탕
59 Beef Tangsuyuk	65 GulJeon	63 떡갈비
66 Haddock Jeon	61 Huin Sal SaengSeonJeon	66 생선전
65 Oyster Jeon	66 SaengSeonJeon	60 소갈비
64 Perilla & Beef Jeon	60 SoGalBi	67 소갈비찜
62 Sea Snail Muchim	67 SoGalBiJjim	55 소고기불고기
58 Spicy Chicken Bokkeumtang	55 SoGoGi BulGoGi	56 소고기완자튀김
54 Spicy Chicken Galbi	56 SoGoGiWanJaTwiGim	68 안동 찜닭
57 Stuffed Pepper Jeon	59 TangSuYuk	69 양념 통닭
69 Sweet & Spicy Tongdak	63 TteokGalBi	59 탕수육
61 White Fish Jeon	69 YangNyeom TongDak	61 흰 살 생선전

Rice & Noodles

84 Beef Deopbap	72 BiBimNaengMyeon	80 굴죽
81 Beef Jumeokbap	86 ChamChiGimChi SamGakGimBap	74 김치볶음밥
76 Beef Kimbap	83 ChamChiMaYo SamGakGimBap	79 김치 비빔국수
90 Black Bean Paste Myeon	70 ChiJeu OBeun SeuPaGeTi	73 김치라면
87 Buckwheat Guksu	85 Dak YaChaeBokkEumBap	85 닭 야채볶음밥
70 Cheese Oven Spaghetti	79 GimChi BiBimGukSu	87 메밀국수
85 Chicken & Veggie Bokkeumbap	74 GimChiBokkEumBap	77 물냉면
77 Cold Buckwheat Guksu	73 GimChiRaMyeon	72 비빔냉면
71 Curry Bap	80 GulJuk	76 소고기 김밥
79 Kimchi Bibimguksu	90 JaJangMyeon	81 소고기 주먹밥
74 Kimchi Bokkeumbap	88 JatJuk	84 소고기덮밥
73 Kimchi Ramyeon	75 JjamBbong	82 야채볶음밥
80 Oyster Juk	71 KaReRaISeu	91 유부초밥
88 Pine Nut Juk	78 KongNaMulBap	90 자장면
89 Red Bean Juk	87 MeMilGukSu	88 잣죽
91 Soybean Curd Chobap	77 MulNaengMyeon	75 짬뽕
78 Soybean Sprout Bap	89 PatJuk	86 참치김치 삼각김밥
72 Spicy Cold Buckwheat Myeon	76 SoGoGi GimBap	83 참치마요 삼각김밥
75 Spicy Seafood Guksu	81 SoGoGi JuMeokBap	70 치즈 오븐 스파게티
86 Tuna Kimchi Triangle Kimbap	84 SoGoGiDeopBap	71 카레라이스
83 Tuna Mayo Triangle Kimbap	82 YaChaeBokkEumBap	78 콩나물밥
82 Veggie Bokkeumbap	91 YuBuChoBap	89 팥죽

Desserts & Drinks

93 Brown Sugar & Cinnamon Hotteok	100 ChapSsalTteok	95 경단
95 Cake Crumb Gyeongdan	98 DaeChu SaengGangCha	99 고구마 맛탕
103 Cannellini Bean Gwaja	104 DanPatBbang	97 꽈배기 도너츠
92 Cinnamon Cha	99 GoGuMa MatTang	94 녹차 아이스크림
98 Date & Ginger Cha	95 GyeongDan	104 단팥빵
102 Dumpling Wrapper Hotteok	93 HoTteok	98 대추 생강차
94 Green Tea Ice Cream	97 KkwaBaeGi DoNeoCheu	102 만두피 호떡
97 Korean Twisted Donuts	102 ManDuPi HoTteok	103 상투과자
96 Red Bean Bingsu	94 NokCha AISeuKeuRim	92 수정과
101 Red Bean Ice Cream	101 Pat AISeuKeuRim	105 식혜
99 Sweet Potato Mattang	96 PatBingSu	100 찹쌀떡
104 Sweet Red Bean Bbang	103 SangTuGwaJa	101 팥 아이스크림
100 Sweet Rice & Red Bean Tteok	105 SikHye	96 팥빙수
105 Sweet Rice Eumryo	92 SuJeongGwa	93 호떡

Potato Jeon

감자전, GamJaJeon

Yield: 8 Pancakes

1$^1/_2$ lbs Potatoes, 1-Inch Cubes
$^1/_4$ tsp Salt
Green Onion, Thinly Sliced (Garnish)
Red Hot Pepper, Finely Diced (Garnish)
Vegetable Oil for Frying

 To prevent the potatoes from turning brown, put them in water while cutting them. Drain when done.

 Grind the potatoes until they become a very fine paste. You can use either a mixer or a hand grinder. Drain with a sieve and save both the ground potato and the potato water.

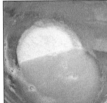 Cover the ground potato with plastic wrap. Set aside the potato water for about 15 minutes.

 The potato starch will settle to the bottom of the potato water. Remove the liquid on top and save only the potato starch.

 Add the potato starch to the potato paste along with $^1/_4$ tsp of salt and mix everything together.

 In a generously oiled and heated pan, add a spoonful of potato mixture and make it round. Place some green onions or peppers on the pancakes.

 Fry them until both sides of the pancakes become golden brown. Garnish with more green onions and hot peppers.

Potato pancakes are an amazingly simple yet delicious snack to eat. This dish has been requested many times on my blog. Interestingly, people who requested it saw this dish on the Korean TV program "Family Outing." In that program, Lee Hyori cooked this in one episode.

Zucchini Jeon

Yield: 2 Servings

애호박전, AeHoBakJeon

INGREDIENTS

2 Cups Zucchini, Julienned	1 Egg
½ Cup Onion, Finely Chopped	½ tsp Salt
1 Tbsp Red Hot Pepper, Finely Chopped	

For the Dipping Sauce
1½ Tbps Soy Sauce
½ tsp Brown Rice Vinegar or Apple Vinegar

For the Batter
1 Cup All-Purpose Flour
1 Cup Water

Mix together the ingredients for the batter in a bowl.

Fry them until they become golden brown. Serve with dipping sauce.

Add the veggies into the batter and then mix everything together.

In a slightly oiled pan, pour 1 large spoonful of the batter and spread it to make a round shape.

Zucchini jeon is one of the many types of jeon in Korea. The soft texture of the zucchini is a good match with the soft inside, and crispy outside, of this jeon. The onions and hot peppers give extra flavor to it. Soy dipping sauce is the perfect addition. This is eaten as a snack or side dish.

Royal Palace Tteokbokki

궁중 떡볶이, GungJung TteokBokkI

Yield: 2 Servings

INGREDIENTS

30	Sticky Rice Cakes (2-Inch)
3	oz ($^1/_3$ Cup) Ground Beef
2	Dried Shiitake Mushrooms
$^2/_3$	Cup Onion, Sliced
$^2/_3$	Cup Sweet Peppers, Sliced
$^1/_4$	Cup Carrot, Julienned
1	Hot Pepper, Sliced (Optional)
1	tsp Sesame Seeds

For the Sauce

3	Tbsp Soy Sauce
$1^1/_2$	Tbsp Sugar
$^1/_2$	Tbsp Garlic, Minced
$1^1/_2$	Tbsp Green Onion, Finely Chopped
1	tsp Sesame Oil
$^1/_8$	tsp Black Pepper
3	Tbsp Shiitake Mushroom Broth or Water

Soak two dried Shiitake mushrooms in water for 10 minutes. Squeeze out the water. Save the broth for later. Remove the stems and slice the mushrooms thinly.

Mix all the ingredients for the sauce together.

Add 2 Tbsp of sauce mixture to the beef and mushrooms, and then mix well. Let it marinate while you are preparing the other ingredients.

Cook frozen rice cakes in boiling water for about 2 minutes, or until soft, and then drain them. Reduce the time for fresh or refrigerated rice cakes. They will absorb the flavor better when they are soft.

In a heated pan, brown the marinated beef and mushrooms on medium. Add the onion and carrot, and then fry for a minute on high.

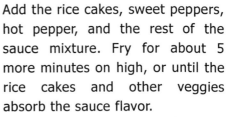
Add the rice cakes, sweet peppers, hot pepper, and the rest of the sauce mixture. Fry for about 5 more minutes on high, or until the rice cakes and other veggies absorb the sauce flavor.

Add 2 Tbsp of mushroom broth or water. This adds moisture and flavor. Shiitake mushrooms have a strong and unique flavor; you may want to use water instead. Garnish with sesame seeds.

Tteokbokki is one of the most popular Korean street foods. This recipe is different from the more common spicy tteokbokki. This is sometimes called "soy sauce tteokbokki," or "ganjang tteokbokki." Legend has it that this originated from a dish that was served for the king or his royal family in Korean history.

Spicy Tteokbokki

Yield: 3 Servings

떡볶이, TteokBokkI

INGREDIENTS

2 Cups (15) Sticky Rice Cake Sticks
2 Fried Fish Cakes (6 oz), 6 x 7 Inch
1 Cup Cabbage, $1/_4$-Inch Pieces
$2/_3$ Cup Onion, $1/_4$-Inch Slices
$1/_2$ Cup Carrot, Diagonally Sliced
1 Green Onion, $1/_2$-Inch Pieces
Sesame Seeds (Garnish)

For the Broth
$2^1/_2$ Cups Water
6 Pieces Dried Kelp, 1 x 2 Inch Pieces
1 Dried Anchovy Pack (Optional)

For the Sauce
3 Tbsp Hot Pepper Paste
1 Tbsp Hot Pepper Powder
2 Tbsp Corn Syrup (or Sugar)
$1/_2$ Tbsp Sugar
1 Tbsp Soy Sauce
$1/_2$ Tbsp Garlic, Minced

To make the broth, boil the ingredients for the broth and the fish cakes together for about 10 minutes.

Remove and save the fish cakes for later. Discard the kelp and anchovy pack. Cut the cooked fish cakes, and the sticky rice cakes, into 2-inch strips.

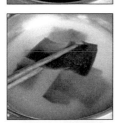

Combine and cook all the sauce ingredients for 5 minutes on medium-high. You can adjust the sugar or hot pepper paste amounts, and/or skip the hot pepper powder.

Add the rice cakes, carrot, onion, and cabbage into the broth. Cook for about 5 minutes, or until the rice cakes become soft, on medium-high.

Add the fish cakes and cook for 1 more minute.

Add the green onion, cook for another minute, and then turn off the heat. Sprinkle some sesame seeds on top, just before serving.

TteokBokkI is one of the most popular Korean street foods. Since it is easy to make, Koreans often make it at home. This snack has many different names according to its ingredients such as cheese TteokBokkI, RaBokkI (Ramen noodles), GanJang TteokBokkI, or GungJung TteokBokkI (soy sauce).

Chicken & Veggie Naengchae

닭가슴살 겨자냉채, DakGaSeumSal GyeoJaNaengChae

Yield: 4 Servings

INGREDIENTS

1	Cup Cooked Chicken Breast, Shredded		1	Tbsp Vinegar
$^1/_3$	Cup Carrot, Julienned		1	Tbsp Lemon Juice
$^1/_3$	Cup Cucumber, Julienned		1	tsp Garlic, Minced
$^1/_3$	Cup Red Cabbage, Julienned		$^1/_8$	tsp Salt
$^1/_3$	Cup Leaf Lettuce, Shredded			
$^1/_3$	Cup Asian Pear or Apple, Julienned			
$^1/_3$	Cup Yellow Sweet Pepper, Julienned			

For the Dressing
$^1/_2$ Tbsp Korean Mustard Paste
2 Tbsp Honey

In a small bowl, mix all the ingredients for the dressing together.

Each guest can pick what they want and mix it together in their own bowl.

Cut the skin off of the cucumber, leaving some of the cucumber on the skin. We will use the part with the skin for our dish. This will make the dish more colorful.

Serve it on a big round plate with the mustard sauce in the center. Arrange the ingredients in groups around the plate.

This is an easy way to serve chicken and veggies with great visual appeal for a party or special meal. The chicken and veggies taste great with the homemade honey mustard dressing. With a little creativity, you can choose different veggies and fruits.

Korean Style Fruit Salad

Yield: $1^1/_2$ Quarts

과일 샐러드, GwaIl SaelReoDeu

INGREDIENTS

1 Cup Red Delicious Apple, $^1/_2$-Inch Cubes	30 Unsalted Peanuts, Peeled
1 Tangerine or Mandarin Orange, Peeled, Divided	$^1/_2$ Cup Crab Sticks, $^1/_2$-Inch Cubes
$^2/_3$ Cup Asian Pear, $^1/_2$-Inch Cubes	$^1/_2$ Cup Mayonnaise
$^2/_3$ Cup Strawberries, Halved	
$^2/_3$ Cup Cucumbers, $^1/_2$-Inch Cubes	
10 Quail Eggs	

Soak the quail eggs in cold water for about 10 minutes. This helps to prevent the eggs from breaking when you boil them later.

Boil the eggs in 2 cups of water and $^1/_2$ tsp of sea salt. Reduce to medium once it starts to boil. The salt and a medium temperature will help prevent the eggs from breaking. Cook for 7 minutes.

Immediately after they finish boiling, drain the hot water and put the eggs in cold water for several minutes. This makes the shells easier to remove. Peel off the eggshells.

Only slightly peel off the cucumber skin. The skin will give your salad extra color.

You can use about 8 cherry tomatoes instead of strawberries.

Add all the ingredients and mayonnaise in a large mixing bowl.

Mix it gently. If you want, you can add a little bit of salt or sugar in this step. I only used mayonnaise for mine. Before serving, chill it in the refrigerator a few minutes; then it will taste even better.

This is an old fashioned food. When mayonnaise was introduced in Korea, this salad was one of the first uses. When people move in Korea, they always have a housewarming party. Almost every party had this salad when I was a kid. My mom also made it for parties at our house. It was one of my favorite menu items. It was fun digging out the best parts: the crab and eggs. Nowadays, it is not as common as before; however, many people still crave it sometimes.

Crabstick Jeon

맛살전, MatSalJeon

Yield: 1 Dozen Pancakes

INGREDIENTS

4	Korean Crab Sticks, Finely Chopped (1 Cup)
3	Eggs, Beaten
$1/3$	Cup Onion, Finely Chopped
1	Green Onion, Finely Chopped
1	Tbsp Carrot, Finely Chopped
1	Red Hot Pepper, Finely Chopped
6	Tbsp All-Purpose Flour
$1/4$	tsp Salt

Add the chopped veggies and crab sticks to the egg mixture and then mix everything together.

Add the flour to the mixture. I mixed all-purpose flour, Korean pancake mix (jeon flour), and frying mix to get better texture. If you do not have them, it is okay to use only normal flour.

Add the salt and mix again.

When you scoop the batter, it should not run off the spoon.

In a oiled pan, put a spoonful of batter and make the shape round. Plenty of oil gives better flavor. Fry them on medium with patience.

When the bottoms become golden brown, flip them over. When the other sides become golden brown, they are done.

This side dish is made with crab sticks, eggs, flour, and different kinds of veggies. Depending on what you have or what you like, you can substitute, add, or delete some of the veggies. You can also use shrimp instead of the crab sticks. This food brings back memories of my school days. When somebody brought this to school, it was very popular with their friends. If you have a chance to make a Korean lunch box for somebody, this is good for it.

Seafood & Green Onion Jeon

Yield: 1 Pancake

해물파전, HaeMulPaJeon

INGREDIENTS

20	Green Onions, 2-Inch Slices
$1/2$	Cup Squid, Rinsed, Bite-Sized Pieces
$1/3$	Cup Medium-Sized Shrimp, Shelled, Rinsed
$1/3$	Cup Mussels, Shelled, Rinsed
$1/3$	Cup Raw Oysters, Rinsed
1	Green Hot Pepper, Thinly Sliced (Optional)
$1/2$	Tbsp All-Purpose Flour
	Vegetable Oil for Frying

For the Batter

$1/2$	Cup Water
$1/4$	Cup All-Purpose Flour
$1/4$	Cup Frying Mix
$1/8$	Generous tsp Salt
1	Egg

Mix all the batter ingredients in a mixing bowl. If you do not have Korean frying mix, just use normal flour instead. Add the seafood and hot pepper into the batter. Mix everything together gently.

Mix about $1/2$ Tbsp of flour into the chopped green onions and mix gently. The flour will help the batter stick to the green onions.

Evenly place the green onions in a heated and generously oiled (about 2 Tbsp) pan.

Pour the seafood mixture on top of the green onions. Spread the batter evenly with a spoon or fork.

Cover and cook for 15 to 20 minutes on medium, or until the top of the pancake is almost done. Since it is thick, and has a lot of seafood, it needs to cook for a long time at a lower temperature.

Flip it over. To make it easier, cover the top with a plate, hold the surface of the plate with your hand, and then turn the pan over with your other hand. Be careful not to burn yourself.

Cleaning the pan will help prevent the pancake from sticking. Add 1 Tbsp of oil. Put the pancake back in the pan. Fry for 5 more minutes. Sometimes shake it to make sure that it does not stick.

Combine 2 Tbsp of soy sauce, 2 tsp of water, and $3/4$ tsp of vinegar to make dipping sauce.

Seafood and green onion pancakes are perfect for seafood lovers like myself. This is one of the most popular foods for festivals in Korea. The awesome taste comes from the different kinds of seafood and green onions, which are fried into a nicely golden-brown crispy pancake. Some people pour the egg on top of the pancake before frying it, but I prefer my egg in the batter. If you increase the salt a little more, you might not need dipping sauce. However, we usually use soy dipping sauce.

Rest Stop Gamja

휴게소감자, HyuGeSoGamJa

Yield: 2 Servings

INGREDIENTS

10	oz Baby Potatoes
2$^1/_3$	Cups Water
1	tsp Salt
2	Tbsp Butter
	Parsley (Garnish)

Prepare the baby potatoes. If you don't have baby potatoes, you can cut normal potatoes into baby potato sized pieces.

Peel the potatoes, and keep them in cold water to prevent them from turning brown while you are peeling the other ones.

Add the water, potatoes, and 1 tsp of salt in a pot. Once the water starts to boil, cook for about 15 to 20 minutes on high.

Poke a potato with a chopstick or fork to see if it is done. If it goes through smoothly they are done. Drain.

Melt the butter in a pan.

Add the cooked potatoes into the heated pan, and fry them on medium-low.

Turn them occasionally so that they brown evenly. They are done when golden brown. Sprinkle a little salt on them if needed. Garnish with parsley. They taste best when they are warm.

In Korea, there are many rest stops along the major highways. The best thing about Korean rest stops is the different kinds of snack foods to try. Rest Stop Gamja is one of the popular rest stop foods. With less than five ingredients, you can make this delicious snack. Potatoes fried in butter, with just the right amount of saltiness, will make your mouth very happy.

Chicken Ggochi

Yield: 8 Skewers

간장 닭꼬치, GanJang DakGgoChi

INGREDIENTS

8	Skewer Sticks (5-Inch)
2	Korean Green Peppers, $1/_2$-Inch Cubes
8	Green Onions, Bottoms of, $1/_2$-Inch Cubes
8	Garlic Cloves

For the Sauce

$2/_3$	Cup Water
$1/_4$	Cup Soy Sauce
2	Tbsp Cooking Wine (or Water)
$1^1/_2$	Tbsp Sugar
2	Garlic Cloves

1	Fingernail Sized Piece of Ginger
$1/_2$	tsp Peppercorns
1	Pinch Hot Pepper Powder (Optional)

For the Chicken

1	Chicken Breast, $1/_2$-Inch Cubes
1	tsp Cooking Wine (or Water)
2	Pinches Salt
2	Pinches Black Pepper

 Mix the chicken ingredients together and let it marinate while you are preparing the other things.

 Combine all the ingredients for the sauce on high. Stir until the sugar dissolves. Once it starts to boil, cook on medium for 5 minutes. Strain the sauce and discard the cooked veggies.

Obtain 8 5-inch bamboo skewers. Place the ingredients on the skewers in the following order: garlic, chicken, pepper, chicken, onion, and then chicken.

 Place the skewers in a heated and generously oiled pan (about 1 Tbsp of vegetable oil), and cook on medium-high. Fry them on each side for about a minute.

 Pour half of the sauce over the skewers and cook for about 5 minutes on high. The sauce will thicken, almost disappearing.

 Flip the skewers over and pour the rest of the sauce on top of them. Cook for another 5 minutes.

There are several kinds of skewered chicken in Korea. This one is made with chicken, garlic, peppers, and green onions, all marinated in a special sauce. It all tastes really good together. You can use more garlic or pepper for each skewer. The peppers are not very spicy and they have a little sweet flavor in their crunchy texture. If you cannot find these Korean peppers, you can use banana peppers, bell peppers, or any other pepper that you like.

Sweet Corn Salad

콘샐러드, ConSaelReoDeu

Yield: 1$\frac{1}{2}$ Cups

INGREDIENTS

1	Can (15 oz) Sweet Corn
2	Tbsp Onion, Finely Chopped
1	Tbsp Green Sweet Pepper, Finely Chopped
1	Tbsp Red Sweet Pepper, Finely Chopped
4	Tbsp Mayonnaise
1	Tbsp Sugar
$\frac{1}{2}$	Tbsp Vinegar
2	Pinches Salt
1	Pinch White or Black Pepper

Drain one can of sweet corn. You will get about 1$\frac{1}{3}$ cups of sweet corn kernels.

Chill it in the refrigerator. Serve it chilled, or the next day.

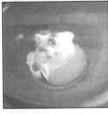
Combine the mayonnaise, sugar, vinegar, salt, and white or black pepper in a mixing bowl. Mix everything together.

Add the sweet corn and other veggies to the sauce. Mix everything together.

This is a popular side dish that Western restaurants such as KFC and Pizza Hut made popular in Korea. It might seem strange since this recipe is not served by those restaurants in the USA, but many Western restaurants change their menu according to local tastes. It is good when eating greasy food. The onion, sweet pepper, and sweet and sour sauce, helps remove the oily taste from your mouth. It also can be good as an appetizer or side for other kinds of food.

Crown Daisy Jeon

Yield: 2 Servings

쑥갓전, SsukGatJeon

1 Cup Crown Daisy, Washed, Drained	2 Eggs
$^1/_2$ Cup Onion, Finely Chopped	$^1/_2$ Generous tsp Salt
1 Tbsp Red Hot Pepper, Thinly Sliced	

For the Batter
1 Cup All-Purpose Flour
$^2/_3$ Cup Water

Combine the ingredients for the batter in a mixing bowl.

Mix the batter gently. You will get a consistency like crêpe batter.

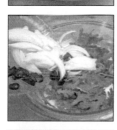

Add the crown daisy, onion, and hot pepper into the batter.

Mix everything together.

Pour half of the batter into a heated and generously oiled 12-inch pan. Spread it out evenly and thinly.

Fry until both sides become golden brown. Press it with your spatula sometimes to make it more crispy and delicious. Serve with dipping sauce.

To make the dipping sauce, combine $1^1/_2$ Tbsp of soy sauce, 1 tsp of water, and $^1/_2$ tsp of vinegar.

Crown daisy, called "ssukgat" in Korean, is an edible chrysanthemum. In Korean cuisine, it is often used because of the unique flavor. It gives extra flavor to some dishes and soups, in the same way some herbs are used in Western cuisine to add flavor. Crown daisy jeon is considered a healthy and tasty Korean pancake.

Spicy Yellow Croaker Maeuntang

조기매운탕, JoGiMaeUnTang

Yield: 3 Servings

INGREDIENTS

3   Yellow Croaker Fish
2   Cups Korean Radish, Peeled, 1 x 2 x $^1/_2$ Inch Pieces
$^1/_2$ Cup Onion, $^1/_2$-Inch Slices
2   Green Onions, $^1/_2$-Inch Slices
1   Hot Pepper, $^1/_2$-Inch Pieces (Optional)

For the Broth
4   Cups Water
1   Dried Anchovy Pack (6 Dried Anchovies)
5   Pieces Dried Kelp (1 x 2 Inch)

For the Seasoning
2   Tbsp Soup Soy Sauce
$1^1/_2$ Tbsp Hot Pepper Oil
1   Tbsp Cooking Wine (or Water)
1   Tbsp Garlic, Minced
$^1/_4$ tsp Ginger, Minced
1   Tbsp Hot Pepper Powder

Rinse the fish, and then cut the tails and fins with scissors. Boil the broth ingredients on medium-high for 10 minutes.

Half way through boiling, remove the kelp from the broth. After the full 10 minutes, remove the anchovy pack.

Add all the seasoning ingredients, minus the hot pepper powder, to the broth. Add the radish and cook for several minutes, covered, until it starts to boil again.

Add the fish and onions.

If you like spicy food, add 1 Tbsp of hot pepper powder. Adjust the saltiness if you want. Cook covered for about 10 minutes on high.

Add the chopped green onions and hot peppers into the soup. Cook 2 more minutes on high and then turn off the heat. Be careful because it is easy to add too much pepper.

Yellow croaker has a strong flavor and slightly chewy texture. The spicy sauce and broth in this soup makes the fish taste pleasant. The cooked radish is also delicious and a good match. In Korea, we like to eat fried croaker, but we also love this spicy soup.

Spicy Mackerel Jorim

Yield: 2 Servings

고등어조림, GoDeungEoJoRim

INGREDIENTS

1	Blue Mackerel, 2-Inch Pieces
1	Cup Korean Radish, 1 x 2 Inch Pieces
$^1/_2$	Cup Onion, $^1/_2$-Inch Slices
1	Green Onion, 1-Inch Pieces
1	Hot Pepper, $^1/_2$-Inch Slices

For the Broth

1	Dried Anchovy Pack (6 Dried Anchovies)
2	Cups Water

For the Sauce

2	Tbsp Hot Pepper Paste (Gochujang)
1	Tbsp Hot Pepper Powder
2	Tbsp Cooking Wine (or Water)
$1^1/_2$	Tbsp Soy Sauce
1	Tbsp Soup Soy Sauce
1	Tbsp Sugar
$^1/_8$	tsp Black Pepper
1	Tbsp Garlic, Minced
$^1/_4$	tsp Ginger, Minced

Add the ingredients for the broth and the radish in a pan.

Once it starts to boil, cook for 5 minutes to make the broth. Then remove the dried anchovies.

Use fresh blue mackerel, not the salted one, for this recipe.

Combine all the ingredients for the sauce in a small bowl. Put the mackerel on top of the radish and pour the sauce on top of the mackerel. Boil until the soup has reduced to half.

Occasionally pour the stew's broth over the fish and radish pieces as it cooks. Add the onion on top of the stew. Cook until the mackerel has completely cooked.

My fish took 10 minutes to cook. Add the green onions and hot peppers. Cook for 2 more minutes.

This dish is a spicy Korean stew using mackerel fish. The flavors of the different ingredients in this stew are awesome together. If you eat this stew, you can finish your rice without any other side dishes. There is research that says the dark flesh of fish, like mackerel, is good for high blood pressure.

Fish Cake Guk

어묵국, EoMukGuk

Yield: 2 Servings

INGREDIENTS

1	Pack of Square Fried Fish Cakes (14 oz), 5 Pieces
5	Skewers
1	Cup Korean Radish, $1^1/_2$ x 2 x $^1/_2$ Inch Pieces
1	Green Onions, $^1/_2$-Inch Pieces
2	Tbsp Soup Soy Sauce
$^1/_8$	tsp Sea Salt

For the Broth

6	Pieces Dried Kelp, 1 x 2 Inch Pieces
1	Green Onions, 2-Inch Pieces
1	Red Hot Pepper, $^1/_2$-Inch Pieces (Optional)
6	Cups Water

In a large pan, add the ingredients for the broth, the radish, and 2 or 3 pieces of the hot pepper. Once it starts to boil, cook for 5 minutes on high.

Fold a third of the square fried fish cake.

Fold the fish cake again.

Start placing the folded fish cake on the skewer.

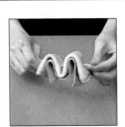

Put the fried fish cake on the skewer stick as pictured.

Remove and discard the kelp and green onions.

Add the skewered fish cakes, soup soy sauce, and salt. Reduce to medium-high and cook for 10 more minutes.

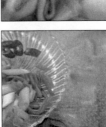

Add the $^1/_2$-inch pieces of green onion and optional hot pepper. Cook for 2 more minutes.

Fried fish cake soup is a street food in Korea. This warm tasty soup is especially good in the cold winter. This tastes even better with some Korean snacks like tteokbokki or kimbap. Try this easy and delicious soup with your family someday.

Haddock Guk

Yield: 2 Servings

동태국, DongTaeGuk

INGREDIENTS

12 oz Haddock, Cubed
$1/_2$ Cup Onion, Sliced
2 Green Onions, $1/_2$-Inch Pieces
$1/_2$ Red Hot Pepper, Sliced
1 tsp Salt
$1/_2$ Tbsp Garlic, Minced
$1/_2$ Cup Korean Radish, Sliced

For the Broth
5 Cups Water
6 Dried Anchovies or 1 Dried Anchovy Pack

6 Pieces Dried Kelp, $1^1/_2$ x 2 Inch

Put the broth ingredients in a medium sized pan. Boil for 10 minutes on medium-high.

Discard the anchovy pack and kelp.

Add the haddock, radish, and onion into the broth. When the soup starts to boil again, add the minced garlic and salt. Cook for another 10 minutes on high.

Occasionally remove the foam that forms on the top of the soup. This will make the broth clear, and it will help to remove the bad fish taste.

Add the hot pepper and green onions. If you don't like spicy food, just add 1 or 2 pieces of hot pepper.

Cook for 2 more minutes. You may want to adjust the amount of salt in this step.

Haddock soup is one of my favorite soups. I learned to make it from my mom. My mom used pollock. You can use either pollock or haddock. Serve this soup with rice and other Korean side dishes.

Extra Soft Tofu Jjigae

순두부찌개, SunDuBuJjiGae   Yield: 2 Servings

INGREDIENTS

1	Pack (11 oz) Extra Soft Tofu (SoonDuBu)
1/4	Cup Kimchi, Bite-Sized Pieces
1/2	Pack Enokitake Mushroom, Stems Cut in Half and Bottoms Discarded
1/3	Cup Zucchini, Quartered Slices
1/2	Cup Onion, 1/2-Inch Pieces
1	Green Onion, 1/2-Inch Pieces
1	Hot Pepper, 1/2-Inch Pieces
1	Egg
1	Tbsp Soup Soy Sauce
	Salt to Taste
	Black Pepper to Taste

For the Beef

2   oz (1/4 Cup) Beef, 1/4 x 1/4 x 2 Inch Strips

1/2   tsp Cooking Wine (or Water)
1/2   tsp Soy Sauce
1/4   tsp Garlic, Minced
1   Pinch Black Pepper

For the Broth

10   Clams
2 1/2   Cups Water
5   Pieces Dried Kelp (1 x 2 inch)

For the Seasoning

2   Tbsp Hot Pepper Powder
1   Tbsp Vegetable Oil
1/2   Tbsp Hot Pepper Oil
1/2   Tbsp Garlic, Minced

Marinate the beef with the cooking wine, soy sauce, garlic, and black pepper while you are preparing the other ingredients.

Rinse the clams once in cold water. To make the broth, cook the clams and kelp in the water for 5 minutes on high. Afterwards, remove the clams and kelp from the broth. Discard the kelp.

Fry the seasoning ingredients together for 10 seconds on high in a heated pan. Add the marinated beef and fry until it is half cooked. Add the onion and kimchi. Fry until the beef is well done.

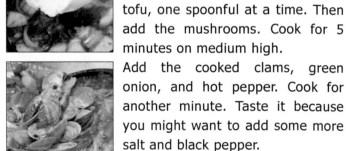

Add the broth, soup soy sauce, and zucchini. Cook on high. Once it starts to boil, add 1 pack of soft tofu, one spoonful at a time. Then add the mushrooms. Cook for 5 minutes on medium high.

Add the cooked clams, green onion, and hot pepper. Cook for another minute. Taste it because you might want to add some more salt and black pepper.

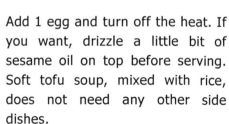

Add 1 egg and turn off the heat. If you want, drizzle a little bit of sesame oil on top before serving. Soft tofu soup, mixed with rice, does not need any other side dishes.

It was amazing to get so many requests for extra soft tofu soup. This shows me that many people in the world like this soup. The broth is spicy and is a good match for the extra soft tofu. With the same basic seasonings used in this soup, you can make different varieties such as beef or clam. The kimchi is optional. You can use shiitake mushrooms, or your favorite mushroom, instead of the Enokitake mushroom.

Tuna Kimchi Jjigae

Yield: 3 Servings

참치 김치찌개, ChamChi GimChiJjiGae

INGREDIENTS

1¹/₂ Cups Kimchi
2 Cups Water
1 Cup Tuna
¹/₂ Pack Tofu (9 oz), ¹/₂-Inch Slices
¹/₄ Cup Onion, ¹/₂-Inch Slices
1 Green Onion, 1-Inch Pieces
¹/₂ Green Hot Pepper, ¹/₂-Inch Pieces
¹/₂ Red Hot Pepper, ¹/₂-Inch Pieces

For the Seasoning
¹/₈ Cup Kimchi Broth

¹/₂ Tbsp Hot Pepper Powder
1 tsp Garlic, Minced
1 tsp Salt

Cut the kimchi into 1-inch pieces. It is important to use well-fermented kimchi for kimchi soup. Sour (old) kimchi works good too.

I recommend tuna packaged In oil instead of water. If you get a Korean tuna can, 1 medium sized can will be enough. Use all the oil and tuna from the can for the soup.

In a pan, add the kimchi and water. Boil it on high. Once the soup starts to boil, add the tuna.

Add the onion and seasoning ingredients. Adjust the amount of salt depending on the saltiness of your kimchi.

If you used tuna packed in water, add 1 Tbsp of vegetable oil. Cook covered for 15 to 20 minutes, or until the kimchi has cooked.

Add the tofu, green onion, and hot peppers. Cook for 5 more minutes and turn off the heat.

It would be weird to hear that somebody does not like kimchi or kimchi soup in Korea, except for maybe young kids. Of course once they grow up, they like it. Kimchi is the most famous Korean food. It is thought to be one of the healthiest foods in the world. There are different types of kimchi soup, depending on the ingredients: tofu, tuna, pork, bean sprout, etc. This is tuna kimchi soup.

Beef & Sea Mustard Guk

소고기 미역국, SoGoGi MiYeokGuk

Yield: 2 Servings

INGREDIENTS

1/2 Cup Dried Sea Mustard (or 1 Cup Fresh)	1 Pinch Black Pepper
3 Cups Water	
	For the Seasoning
For the Meat	1/2 Generous Tbsp Garlic, Minced
1/3 Cup Beef, Finely Chopped	1/8 tsp Salt
1 Tbsp Soup Soy Sauce	1/2 Tbsp Sesame Oil
1 tsp Sesame Oil	1/2 Tbsp Soup Soy Sauce

Soak the dried sea mustard for 10 minutes. It will absorb some water and become about 1 cup. Drain.

Cut the soaked sea mustard into bite sized pieces.

In a pan, add the beef along with the meat ingredients. Fry until the beef is almost cooked on medium high.

Add the sea mustard and 1/2 Tbsp of sesame oil. Fry for about 3 minutes on high, or until the beef is completely cooked.

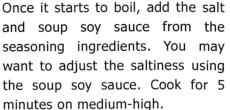
Pour the water into the pan.

Once it starts to boil, add the salt and soup soy sauce from the seasoning ingredients. You may want to adjust the saltiness using the soup soy sauce. Cook for 5 minutes on medium-high.

Add the garlic. Cook for another 5 minutes and then turn off the heat.

Korean people eat this soup anytime, but especially on special days like birthdays, weaning days, etc. This is a beef version, but you can use tuna, clam, mushroom, no meat, etc. Sea mustard is nutritious. It is common for moms to eat this soup after they birth their babies. Also, there is a superstition: Some people will not eat this near an important date for fear of getting bad luck - as to fall down, drop, or fail the test. Sea mustard has a slippery surface; this can imply that somebody will fall down.

Army Base Jjigae

Yield: 3 Servings

부대찌개, BuDaeJjiGae

INGREDIENTS

1	Cup Oval Rice Cakes, Soaked In Water
$1/2$	Cup Well Fermented Kimchi, Bite-Sized Pieces
$1/2$	Cup Onion, $1/4$-Inch Slices
$1/2$	Cup Button Mushrooms, $1/4$-Inch Slices
$1/2$	Pack Ramyeon Noodles
$1/4$	Pack Tofu (4 oz), $1/4$-Inch Slices
$1/4$	Cup Canned Beans, Drained
$1/4$	Cup Ground Beef or Pork
$1/2$	Can Spam, $1/4$-Inch Slices
3	Hotdogs or Sausages, Diagonally Sliced
1	Slice American Cheese (Optional)
2	Green Onions, Chopped 1-Inch Pieces
1	Hot Pepper (Optional), Thinly Sliced

For the Broth

6	Cups Water
1	Dried Anchovy Pack (or 6 Dried Anchovies)
3	Pieces Dried Kelp (1 x 1 Inch Each)

For the Sauce

2	Tbsp Hot Pepper Powder
1	Tbsp Hot Pepper Paste
1	Tbsp Soy Sauce
1	Tbsp Garlic, Minced
1	Tbsp Cooking Wine (or Water)
$1/8$	tsp Black Pepper

Add all the ingredients for the broth in a pot. Boil on medium-high.

Once the broth starts to boil, cook for 5 minutes, and then remove the kelp. Boil for another 5 minutes and take out the anchovy pack.

Place the hot dogs, onion, kimchi, spam, tofu, mushrooms, and beans into the broth in clumps. Place the ground beef in the center of the pot. Mix all the sauce ingredients together.

Spread the rice cakes over the top. Pour the sauce on top of the beef. Once the soup is boiling, stir the beef with a spoon so that it does not cook into a solid chunk. Cook for 10 minutes on high.

Place the noodles, green onions, and hot peppers on top of the soup. Cook for 3 to 5 minutes on high, or until the noodles are cooked.

Place 1 slice of cheese on top of the soup and turn off the heat. Cover it with a lid and let it set a little until the cheese melts. The cheese is optional; I personally prefer mine without cheese.

Army base soup originated during and after the Korean War, when Koreans had very little to eat. People made this dish by combining leftover Spam and hot dogs from U.S. Army facilities, and mixed in with whatever else was available. All the leftovers were combined with water in a large pot and boiled. Nowadays, most Koreans have enough to eat, but this soup is still very popular with more varied ingredients added to it.

Soybean Sprout Guk

콩나물국, KongNaMulGuk   Yield: 2 Servings

INGREDIENTS

7	oz (2 Handfuls) Soybean Sprouts
4	Cups Water
1	Dried Anchovy Pack (or 6 Dried Anchovies)
3	Pieces Dried Kelp (1 x $^1/_2$ Inch)
1	Green Onion, $^1/_2$-Inch Slices
$^1/_2$	Tbsp Soup Soy Sauce
1	tsp Garlic, Minced
$^1/_2$	tsp Salt
$^1/_4$	tsp Hot Pepper Powder (Optional)

Remove any bad parts from both ends of the soybean sprouts and rinse them in cold water.

Add the water, the soybean sprouts, kelp, and dried anchovies in a pot.

Cook covered on medium-high. It is important not to open the lid while it is boiling or you will get bad flavor in your soup.

Once it starts to boil, cook for 5 minutes and then remove the kelp. You may also want to remove the anchovies in this step for a less strong anchovy flavor.

Add the soup soy sauce, garlic, salt, and optional hot pepper powder to the soup. Cook for another 5 minutes on medium-high.

Remove the anchovies. Add the chopped green onion and cook for 2 more minutes. Then, turn off the heat.

Soybean sprout guk is the most common daily soup in Korea. Since it is very quick and simple to make, and the flavor is mild, it is popular as a Korean breakfast soup. Some people say that it is good for a hangover. There are different versions of soybean sprout soup; this recipe is a basic version. Serve it with cooked rice and other Korean side dishes.

Mussel Tang

Yield: 2 Servings

홍합탕, HongHabTang

INGREDIENTS

1	lb Mussels
3	Cups Water
2	Green Onions, $1/2$-Inch Slices
$1/2$	tsp Salt

Wash the mussels in cold water. They might be dirty, so thoroughly clean them.

Add the water and mussels in a pot. Boil on medium-high.

Once it starts to boil, add the salt and cook for 4 more minutes.

When the mussels are almost cooked, add the green onions.

Cook for 1 or 2 more minutes, or until the mussels are completely cooked. When the shells open, they are done. Add salt to taste.

This is one of the easiest Korean soups to make. It is amazing to get such great flavor with such few ingredients. This reminds me of fond childhood memories. Once my mom bought a big bag full of fresh mussels from the market and made this. I was amazed by the huge amount, but as you know, the actual amount of meat inside isn't that much. We finished it all in one sitting. When I eat this, I enjoy not only the taste, but also the memories. Try this someday, and make memories with ones you love.

Oyster Rice Cake Guk

굴떡국, GulTteokGuk   Yield: 2 Servings

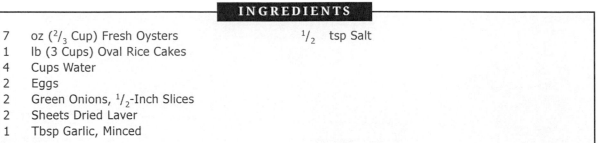

INGREDIENTS

7 oz (²/₃ Cup) Fresh Oysters	¹/₂ tsp Salt
1 lb (3 Cups) Oval Rice Cakes	
4 Cups Water	
2 Eggs	
2 Green Onions, ¹/₂-Inch Slices	
2 Sheets Dried Laver	
1 Tbsp Garlic, Minced	

Rinse the oysters in cold water once and drain.

Pour the water into a pot, and then add the oysters.

Occasionally remove the foam from the surface of the broth; doing that helps to improve the flavor.

Once the broth starts to boil, add the rice cakes. Because of the rice cakes, the temperature of the soup will go down.

When the soup starts to boil again, add the garlic and salt. Cook for about 12 minutes on medium-high, or until the rice cakes become soft.

Mix 2 eggs together and add 2 pinches of salt. Drizzle a little oil on a nonstick pan. Wipe the surface with a paper towel gently. Pour the egg in the pan and cook on low, until both sides are done. Cool the egg and cut it into thin strips. Slice two roasted dried laver sheets into thin strips with scissors.

You may want to adjusted the saltiness with salt or fish sauce. Add the green onion. Cook for 2 more minutes. Pour some into a serving bowl. Garnish it with the egg and laver. Mix before eating.

This rice cake soup is one of my favorite Korean meals. We usually eat this soup on New Year's Day, but you can eat it anytime you want. You can make the soup with different kinds of meat such as beef or oysters. This recipe uses oysters; the same way my mom usually made it for us.

Spicy Beef & Veggie Guk

Yield: 6 Servings

육개장, YukGaeJang

INGREDIENTS

$^1/_2$ lb Beef Brisket
4 Green Onions, 2-Inch Slices
$1^1/_2$ Handfuls Mung Bean Sprouts, Boiled 5 Minutes
1 Handful Dried Fernbrake, Soaked and Boiled ($1^1/_2$ Cups Soaked Fernbrake), 2-Inch Pieces
1 Handful Dried Taro Stems, Soaked and Boiled (1 Cup Soaked Taro Stems), 2-Inch Pieces
$^1/_2$ Cup Onion, $^1/_2$-Inch Pieces
1 Egg, Beaten

For the Broth
10.5 Cups ($2^1/_2$ Liters) Water

5 Garlic Cloves
2 Green Onions, Halved
$^1/_2$ Cup Onion
7 Black Peppercorns

For the Sauce
$3^1/_2$ Tbsp Hot Pepper Powder
3 Tbsp Hot Pepper Oil
3 Tbsp Soup Soy Sauce
$1^1/_2$ Tbsp Sesame Oil
$1^1/_2$ Tbsp Garlic, Minced
$^1/_8$ tsp Black Pepper
1 tsp Sea Salt

Add all the broth ingredients and the beef into a pot. Boil for 40 to 50 minutes on medium-high. Beef brisket is the best cut to use for this soup.

Occasionally, remove the foam from the surface of the broth. When the beef has completely cooked, remove the beef from the broth.

Drain the broth. Discard the other cooked veggies. Tear apart the beef thinly with your fingers. Boiled brisket is easy to pull apart. You may need to use a knife, depending on your cut of beef.

Combine the sauce ingredients. In a large pan, add the meat, veggies, and sauce. Mix it all together and then set it aside for 20 minutes to marinate. Then fry it for about 5 minutes on high.

Pour the broth into the pan. Cook for 20 minutes on medium high.

Reduce to medium. Slowly pour the egg on top. Distribute the egg all around. Don't stir too much, or your broth will not be clear. Boil for several minutes, or until the egg is done.

You may have tried this before, or at least saw it on a menu. It is popular for those who like spicy food. The great flavor comes from the mix of veggies and the homemade broth. When somebody dies in Korea, we visit the house to morn and comfort the family. Visitors usually start arriving 2 or 3 days before the funeral. Hosts serve food to the guests, and nowadays, this is a common soup to serve. Of course, we enjoy eating this soup other times as well, especially in cold weather.

Beef & Radish Guk

소고기 무국, SoGoGi MuGuk

Yield: 4 Servings

INGREDIENTS

1	lb Korean Radish, 1-Inch Cubes
5	Cups Water
2	Green Onions, 2-Inch Slices
3	Tbsp Soup Soy Sauce
1/2	Tbsp Sesame Oil
1/4	tsp Salt

3	tsp Soup Soy Sauce
1	tsp Cooking Wine (or Water)
1/2	tsp Sesame Oil
1/4	tsp Black Pepper

For the Beef

5	oz Beef Brisket, Thin Strips
2	Tbsp Green Onions, Finely Chopped
1	Tbsp Garlic, Minced

Combine the beef ingredients. Set aside for at least 10 minutes to marinate.

Add the sesame oil, the marinated beef, and the radish in a heated pot. Fry it for about 3 minutes on medium-high.

Pour the water into the pot. Once the soup starts to boil, cook for another 13 minutes on high.

Occasionally, remove the foam from the surface of the soup.

Add the soup soy sauce. Taste it and add about 1/4 tsp of salt. You can adjust the saltiness.

Add the chopped green onions and cook for 2 more minutes.

Beef and radish guk is a Korean soup that is eaten daily. This can be good for people who like Korean food, but cannot eat spicy food. The marinated beef and radish gives great flavor to the broth, and the texture of cooked radish with tender beef is good together. Serve it with rice and other Korean side dishes.

Simple Sujaebi

Yield: 3 Servings

수제비, SuJeBi

INGREDIENTS

1	Cup Potato, Bite-Sized Pieces
1	Cup Zucchini, Bite-Sized Pieces
$^1/_2$	Cup Carrot, Bite-Sized Pieces
$^1/_2$	Cup Onion, Bite-Sized Pieces
1	Green Onion, Bite-Sized Pieces

For the Dough

2	Cups All-Purpose Flour
1	Egg
$^1/_2$	Cup Water
$^1/_2$	Tbsp Sea Salt
1	Tbsp Vegetable Oil

For the Broth

6	Cups Water
6	Pieces Dried Kelp (1 x 2 Inch)
1	Dried Anchovy Pack (or 6 Dried Anchovies)

For the Seasoning

$^1/_2$	Tbsp Garlic, Minced
$1^1/_2$	tsp Sea Salt
$1^1/_2$	tsp Soup Soy Sauce
$^1/_2$	Tbsp Sesame Oil

Combine and mix all the dough ingredients. Knead it for about 5 to 10 minutes, until it becomes soft, as in the picture. Cover it with plastic wrap and then set it aside for 30 minutes.

Boil all the broth ingredients for 10 minutes, and then remove the kelp and anchovies.

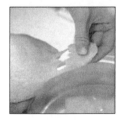

Add the potato into the broth. Squeeze and break off a piece of the dough and add it to the broth. 1-inch pieces will be good. Once it starts to boil, cook for 5 minutes.

Add the onion, carrots, and zucchini. Add all the seasoning ingredients except the sesame oil.

Wait until the dough has cooked. It took mine about 15 minutes. Then add the green onions. Continue cooking for 1 more minute, and then turn off the heat.

Before serving, add the sesame oil (optional). You can adjust the amount of salt and sesame oil. I used a sliced dried hot pepper for my garnish.

Sujaebi is a traditional Korean soup made with dough and veggies. This recipe uses kelp and anchovies for the broth, but you can also use clams or kimchi (or other spicy seasonings). I like sujaebi with clam the most. On a rainy day, cook sujaebi and eat it while watching the rain, it tastes better that way. :) Sometimes Korean people want to eat certain Korean dishes on rainy days such as sujaebi, jeon, or buchimgae.

Spinach Namul

시금치나물, SiGeumChiNaMul

Yield: 2 Servings

INGREDIENTS

3	Handfuls Fresh Spinach (1 Cup Boiled)
7	Cups Water
1	tsp Sesame Oil
1	tsp Garlic, Minced
	Salt
	Sesame Seeds (Garnish)

 Add 1 tsp of sea salt in the water and boil on high. The salt helps the spinach retain its color.

 In the boiling water, add the spinach and cook for 30 seconds on high.

 For the best results, the spinach should be cooked for a short time at a high temperature.

 After 30 seconds, quickly drain and rinse the spinach in cold water several times. This step again helps to retain the green color.

 Squeeze out the water.

 Mix together the boiled spinach, $1/8$ tsp of salt, the sesame oil, and the minced garlic. Garnish with some sesame seeds.

This is one of the many Korean spinach side dishes. Asides from eating this as a side, you can use this for Korean dishes like Bibimbap, JapChae, KimBap, etc.

Mung Bean Sprout Namul

Yield: 1 Pint

숙주나물, SukJuNaMul

INGREDIENTS

14	oz (4 Cups) Mung Bean Sprouts, Washed
5	Cups Water
1	Tbsp Green Onion, Finely Chopped
$^1/_2$	Tbsp Garlic, Minced
$^1/_2$	Tbsp Sesame Seeds
1	Tbsp Sesame Oil
1	tsp Salt

AERI'S TIPS

- The salt will pull water out of the mung bean sprouts and ruin your dish. So for best results, it is important to salt the sprouts, set them aside for a while, and then squeeze any water out of them.

Boil the mung bean sprouts for about 5 to 6 minutes on high.

Drain the water, and let them cool down.

Once they become a little cooler, mix in the salt and set them aside for 10 minutes.

Squeeze out the water.

Add the green onion, garlic, sesame seeds, and sesame oil.

Mix everything together and taste it. You can add a little more salt.

This is a rather healthy Korean side dish made with mung bean sprouts. It is similar to the bean sprout side dish "kong namul." Mung bean sprouts are very perishable, so it is best to eat this dish right after you make it, although you can keep it in the refrigerator for a day or two. Serve this with rice, soup, and other Korean side dishes.

Shredded Cabbage Muchim

양배추무침, YangBaeChuMuChim   Yield: 1 Quart

INGREDIENTS

4	Cups Cabbage, Thinly Sliced
2	Green Onions, Sliced
2	Tbsp Hot Pepper Powder
$1^1/_2$	Tbsp Brown Rice Vinegar or Apple Vinegar
1	Tbsp Sesame Seeds
2	tsp Sugar
2	tsp Sesame Oil
$^1/_2$	tsp Salt
$^1/_2$	tsp Garlic Powder

Combine all the veggies and seasonings in a bowl.

Mix everything together. Store it in the refrigerator.

Shredded cabbage muchim is a simple Korean side dish that I learned to make from one of my Korean friends in America. When you want to eat Kimchi, but don't have it, this cabbage side dish can be a substitute. The taste is a little spicy, sour, and sweet. Cabbage is a healthy veggie; it is reportedly especially good for your stomach. Serve it with rice and other Korean side dishes.

Bellflower Root Muchim

Yield: $^2/_3$ Quarts

도라지무침, DoRaJiMuChim

INGREDIENTS

1 Handful Dried Bellflower Roots (or 1$^1/_2$ Cup Fresh)	$^1/_2$ Tbsp Green Onions, Chopped
$^1/_2$ Cup Cucumber, Diagonally Sliced	$^1/_2$ tsp Salt
2$^1/_2$ Tbsp Hot Pepper Powder	1 tsp Sesame Oil
3 Tbsp Sugar	1 tsp Sesame Seeds
3 Tbsp Brown Rice Vinegar or Apple Vinegar	
$^1/_2$ Tbsp Garlic, Minced	

AERI'S TIPS

- If you use fresh bellflower roots, you have to soak them in water for several hours. You will need about 1$^1/_2$ cup of bellflower roots for this recipe.
- Bellflower roots are a little bitter; soaking them in water helps to reduce the bitterness.

Soak about 1 handful of dried bellflower roots in water over night, or longer. Afterwords, rinse them several times before using.

Mix everything together.

Combine and mix all the ingredients except for the sesame oil.

Add the sesame oil.

This particular side is good for eating by itself or in BiBimBap. It is spicy and has a little sweet and sour flavor to it. Bellflower roots might not be familiar to you. In Korea, they are thought to be good for colds, coughing, and for bringing back your appetite if you loose it. You can make a soup, salad, or side dish with them.

Garlic Chive Kimchi

부추김치, BuChuGimChi

Yield: 1¹/₂ Quarts

INGREDIENTS

1¹/₄ lbs (10 Cups) Garlic Chives
1¹/₃ Cup Onion, Thinly Sliced
3 Tbsp Red Hot Pepper, Thinly Sliced

2 Tbsp Sugar
1¹/₂ Tbsp Garlic, Minced
1¹/₂ Tbsp Sesame Seeds

For the Rice Sauce
3 Tbsp Sweet Rice Flour
1¹/₂ Cup Water

For the Seasoning
¹/₂ Cup Fish Sauce
²/₃ Cup Hot Pepper Powder

Add the rice sauce ingredients in a pan. Mix well to dissolve the flour. You can use normal flour if you don't have sweet rice flour.

Boil it on medium-high, until it starts to make bubbles. Cool it down while you are preparing the other ingredients.

Remove any bad parts from both ends of the garlic chives and rinse them. Cut the garlic chives into about 2-inch lengths.

Combine and mix the seasoning ingredients with 1 cup of cooled rice sauce. The fish sauce will change the saltiness, so use with care.

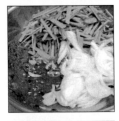
Add the garlic chives, onions, and peppers into the kimchi paste. Mix them all together gently.

Unlike the other kimchi recipes, this one goes directly into the refrigerator because it ferments faster.

Garlic chive kimchi is one of my favorite types of kimchi. This recipe doesn't require soaking in a brine, which makes it easier and quicker to make. Garlic chives have their own unique flavor and they are thought to be healthy. You can eat this fresh or fermented.

Cucumber Kimchi

Yield: 24 Servings

오이소박이, OISoBakI

INGREDIENTS

24	Pickling Cucumbers (About 3-Inches Long), Cleaned
1	Cup Coarse Sea Salt
10	Cups Water
2	Cups Garlic Chives, $^1/_4$-Inch Slices
1	Cup Green Onions, $^1/_4$-Inch Slices

For the Sauce

1	Cup Hot Pepper Powder
6	Tbsp Fish Sauce (or a little Salt)
6	Tbsp Water
2	Tbsp Sugar
2	Tbsp Garlic, Minced
2	tsp Ginger, Minced

 Cut off both ends of the cucumbers. Then cut an X in the cucumbers, lengthwise, all the way down to about half an inch from the bottom.

 Boil the water and salt together. Pour the boiling water on the cucumbers. Set them aside for about 50 minutes. This helps them stay crunchy. Then drain them and rinse them in cold water once.

Mix together the sauce ingredients.

 Mix in the garlic chives and green onions.

 To fill a cucumber with sauce, open the cucumber gently.

 Put some of the sauce mixture in it.

 Rub the surface of the cucumber with the sauce.

Put your cucumber kimchi in a container. I prefer to use glass containers to keep my kimchi. Let them set at room temperature overnight, and then put them in the refrigerator.

Cucumber kimchi is a refreshing summer food in Korea since summer is the best time of year for the fresh cucumbers. On hot summer days, mix rice with cold water and eat this kimchi together for a delicious and refreshing treat. It tastes great both when it is fresh or fermented. In Korea, we use a cucumber called "summer cucumber" for this kimchi. They have a light color and they are thin. I could not find them in the USA, but pickling cucumbers worked well.

Potato Jorim

감자조림, GamJaJoRim

Yield: 2 Servings

INGREDIENTS

2	Cups Potatoes, $1/_2$-Inch Cubes
$1/_2$	Cup Water
2	Tbsp Vegetable Oil
$2^1/_2$	Tbsp Soy Sauce
2	Tbsp Corn Syrup
1	Tbsp Sugar
1	Tbsp Garlic, Minced
$1/_8$	tsp Fine Sea Salt
$1/_2$	tsp Sesame Seeds

 Fry the potatoes in the oil in a preheated pan for 5 minutes on medium-high until they are about a third cooked.

 Add the water, soy sauce, corn syrup, sugar, and garlic. Cook for 5 more minutes on medium-high.

 Taste it, and if you need to, add up to $1/_8$ tsp of fine sea salt. Cook until the liquid is reduced to a paste, which should take about 5 minutes.

 Reduce the temperature to medium and fry 5 to 7 more minutes, or until the potatoes are completely cooked. Then add the sesame seeds.

This is an easy and delicious non-spicy Korean side dish using potatoes. The flavor of soy sauce mixed with a little sweetness and the texture of potatoes gives you a great taste. Although you can make a small amount of this side dish for one meal, you can also make a lot and keep it in the fridge. It is a popular side dish for school lunch boxes in Korea. This tastes good whether it is warm or cool. Serve it with rice and other Korean side dishes.

Tofu Jorim

Yield: 3 Servings

두부조림, DuBuJoRim

INGREDIENTS

1 Pack Firm Tofu (18 oz)	**For the Sauce**
$^1/_3$ Cup Cornstarch or All-Purpose Flour	2 Tbsp Soy Sauce
$^1/_4$ Cup Onion, Finely Chopped	3 Tbsp Water
$^1/_4$ Cup Carrot, Finely Chopped	$2^1/_2$ tsp Sugar
$^1/_4$ Cup Green Onion, Finely Chopped (2 Green onions)	1 Tbsp Garlic, Minced
Vegetable Oil for Frying	1 Tbsp Sesame Oil
Salt and Black Pepper	1 tsp Sesame Seeds
	1 Pinch Black Pepper

Rinse the tofu in water once, and then pad off the water with a paper towel.

Divide the tofu in half and then slice it into $^1/_2$-inch pieces.

Sprinkle some salt and black pepper on both sides of the sliced tofu. Set it aside while you are preparing the other ingredients. This process helps pull the water out of the tofu and give it flavor.

Mix together the sauce ingredients along with the onion, carrot, and green onions.

Cover the tofu with some cornstarch. You can use flour instead, but I personally prefer to use cornstarch for better flavor and texture.

In a heated nonstick pan, add $1^1/_2$ Tbsp of oil, and then place the tofu in the pan. Fry both sides of the tofu until they become golden brown on medium-high.

In a heated pan or wok, add the fried tofu and sauce. Fry for 5 minutes on high. Occasionally stir gently. Be careful not to break the tofu.

About 5 minutes later, the sauce will thicken.

Tofu jorim is an easy and delicious non-spicy side using tofu. The flavor of the soy sauce mixes with the sweetness of the other veggies to give you a great taste. It is best to make a small amount of this side dish: only enough for one meal. Serve when it is warm. Eat it with rice, soup, and other Korean side dishes. You can also eat it as a main dish if you want.

Seaweed Stem Bokkeum

미역줄기볶음, MiYeokJulGiBokkEum

Yield: $^1/_2$ Quart

INGREDIENTS

7   oz (2 Cups) Salted Seaweed Stems
$^1/_8$ Cup Onion, Thinly Sliced
$1^1/_2$ Tbsp Green Onions, Finely Chopped
$^1/_2$ Tbsp Garlic, Minced
$^1/_4$ tsp Sugar
$^1/_2$ tsp Sesame Oil
$^1/_2$ tsp Sesame Seeds
     Some Vegetable Oil for Frying

Rinse the salted seaweed stems to remove the salt. Then wash them about 5 to 6 more times. Soak them in water overnight to leech out more salt. If you skip this step, they will be too salty to eat.

The next day, wash the seaweed stems again and then drain the water. If the stems are too thick, divide them with your fingers. Cut the divided stems into 2 to 3 inch lengths.

Add some oil in a pan on medium heat. After the pan has heated, add the minced garlic and fry for 10 seconds.

Add the seaweed stems and fry for 5 minutes.

Add the onion and green onion. Fry until the onion has completely cooked.

Add the sugar and sesame oil. Taste it and add a little bit of salt, if needed. Lastly, turn off the heat and add the sesame seeds. Stir.

There are many different kinds of sea plants. Among them, this seaweed stem has one of the best tastes and unique textures. Once it is cooked properly, it looses its bad taste and has a delicious savory flavor. The fried garlic in this recipe is critical in that point. It is a little chewy. It is also considered to be a healthy food in Korea. Once you make this, you can keep it in the refrigerator and eat it anytime with rice.

Seasoned Filefish Bokkeum

Yield: 2 Cups

쥐포볶음, JwiPoBokkEum

INGREDIENTS

6	oz (2 Cups) Seasoned Filefish	
$1^1/_2$	Tbsp Hot Pepper Paste	
$^1/_2$	Tbsp Hot Pepper Powder	
$1^1/_2$	Tbsp Vegetable Oil	
1	Tbsp Corn Syrup	
1	Tbsp Onion, Minced	
1	Tbsp Cooking Wine (or Water)	
$^1/_2$	Tbsp Sugar	
$^1/_2$	Tbsp Garlic, Minced	
1	tsp Sesame Seeds	
$^1/_2$	tsp Soy Sauce	

Obtain the seasoned filefish. You can buy them precut in small round shapes, or you can buy big pieces and cut them into bite-sized pieces.

Rinse the fish pieces in cold water once and drain the water. This helps reduce the strong fish smell and clean them.

In a heated pan, fry the fish pieces for about 5 minutes on medium-high, or until they get lightly golden brown. Occasionally stir them so that they will not burn.

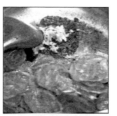

Push the fish aside. Quickly add and mix the oil, hot pepper powder, and garlic together in the pan. Fry for 10 seconds. Pepper powder burns easily, so prepare your ingredients ahead of time.

Add the hot pepper paste, corn syrup, onion, cooking wine, sugar, and soy sauce. Mix up the sauce and then mix the sauce into the fish.

Fry for about 5 minutes on medium-high. Turn off the heat. Sprinkle sesame seeds on top and mix.

Seasoned filefish bokkeum is one of the most common side dishes that mothers like to keep in the fridge and serve with each meal. It keeps for several weeks. You can substitute dried anchovies or dried shrimp using the same sauce that I use in this recipe. The sauce is spicy and sweet which goes well with the salted, dried fish. Keep it in the refrigerator and serve it cool whenever you eat your meals.

Baby Potato Jorim

알감자조림, AlGamJaJoRim

Yield: 5 Servings

INGREDIENTS

1¹/₄ lbs Little Baby Potatoes, Cleaned, Drained
4   Cups Water
¹/₂ Cup Soy Sauce
4   Tbsp Corn Syrup
2   Tbsp Sugar
1   Tbsp Cooking Wine (or Water)
1   tsp Sesame Seeds

AERI'S TIPS

- They taste best right after cooking, so I recommend that you don't make too much.

 Boil the potatoes for about 15 to 20 minutes on high, or until they are half cooked, in a large pan. The water should be reduced to about half.

 Turn off the heat, and sprinkle sesame seeds on top.

 Add the soy sauce, corn syrup, sugar, and cooking wine.

 Cook on medium for about 25 to 30 minutes, or until the potatoes are fully cooked. The sauce will be thicker.

This recipe is a good side for making large batches and serving for several days at each meal. When you cook the potatoes in soy sauce and sugar, the skin gets a nice chewy texture and absorbs the soy sauce and sugar flavors. The insides are soft. This dish is good both warm and cold.

Zucchini Bokkeum

Yield: 1 Pint

애호박볶음, AeHoBakBokkEum

2	Cups Zucchini, Thinly Sliced
1	tsp Sea Salt
1	Tbsp Vegetable Oil
$^1/_2$	Tbsp Sesame Oil
1	tsp Sesame Seeds
1	Tbsp Green Onion, Finely Chopped
1	tsp Garlic, Minced

AERI'S TIPS

• The salt will pull the water out of the zucchini and give it flavor. Also, when you cook it later, your zucchini will not be watery. (You don't want soft and mushy zucchini.)

 Mix the salt in the zucchini, and set it aside for about 30 minutes.

 When the zucchini has almost finished cooking, add the garlic, green onions, sesame oil, and sesame seeds. Fry 2 more minutes and then turn off the heat. You may want to add more salt.

 You will get liquid from the zucchini. Squeeze out the water.

 In a pan, add the oil. When the pan is heated, add the zucchini and fry for 7 minutes on medium.

Zucchini bokkeum is a simple Korean side. The natural zucchini flavor shines in this dish with a hint of the garlic, green onions, salt, sesame oil, and sesame seeds. This is a common flavor that you can taste in Korean dishes. It is good when added to bibimbap.

Pickled Cucumber Muchim

오이지무침, OIJiMuChim

Yield: 1 Pint

INGREDIENTS

2	Cups Korean Pickled Cucumbers, Thinly Sliced
2	Tbsp Hot Pepper Powder
$1/_2$	Tbsp Sugar
2	Tbsp Sesame Oil
1	Tbsp Garlic, Minced
2	Tbsp Green Onions, Finely Chopped

$1/_2$ Tbsp Sesame Seeds

AERI'S TIPS

• Try this someday: mix your rice with cold water, and eat it with this side dish. It is good for a hot summer day's lunch, when you feel lazy to cook.

Rinse the chopped pickled cucumbers in cold water once.

Add the pickled cucumbers and the rest of the ingredients in a mixing bowl. Mix everything together.

Drain the water.

Squeeze out the water.

This is a pickled cucumber side dish. You can make your own pickled cucumbers at home; you can also simply buy pickled cucumbers in a Korean or Asian store. This is simple to make and it can be used in all four seasons; however, it is especially good during the summer.

Perilla Kimchi

Yield: 6$\frac{1}{2}$ Dozen Leaves

깻잎김치, GgaetIpGimChi

INGREDIENTS

80   Perilla Leaves (a.k.a. Sesame Leaves), Washed, Drained

1$\frac{1}{2}$ Tbsp Asian Pear (Optional), Ground

For the Paste

1$\frac{1}{2}$ Tbsp Sugar

1   Tbsp Garlic, Minced

1   Tbsp Sesame Seeds

$\frac{1}{2}$ tsp Ginger, Minced

$\frac{1}{4}$ Cup Fish Sauce

3   Tbsp Water

$\frac{1}{3}$ Cup Green Onions, Finely Chopped

$\frac{1}{4}$ Cup Carrot, Julienned

$\frac{1}{2}$ Cup Hot Pepper Powder

AERI'S TIPS

- Leave the kimchi at room temperature for half a day and then store it in the refrigerator. It will be ready to eat in 2 to 3 days.
- Serve it with rice, soup, and other Korean side dishes.

Combine the ingredients for the paste. Mix everything together.

You may want to adjust the sweetness with sugar or ground pear, the spiciness with hot pepper powder, and the saltiness with salt or fish sauce. I like to add ground Asian pear.

Place one perilla leaf on a plate and spread some kimchi paste evenly on top of it. Repeat this for each leaf. Make separate stacks of 10 to 15 leaves.

Arrange the stacks of leaves inside a glass container in different directions so that they will be nicely spaced out. It will help make it easier to take them out later when you eat the kimchi.

Perilla kimchi is a simple type of kimchi. It does not need to soak in a brine like normal kimchi and it does not need to ferment very long. So even though it called kimchi, it is almost like a daily side dish. Perilla has a unique taste, and it is thought to be good for health. This kimchi tastes great both when it is fresh and fermented.

Cucumber Naengguk

오이냉국, OINaengGuk

Yield: 1¹/₂ Quarts

INGREDIENTS

2	Cups Cucumbers, Julienned
1¹/₂	Cups Water
1¹/₂	Tbsp Green Onions, Finely Chopped
1	tsp Green Hot Pepper (Optional), Finely Chopped
1	tsp Red Hot Pepper (Optional), Finely Chopped

For the Seasoning

2	Tbsp Brown Rice Vinegar or Apple Vinegar
2	Tbsp Sugar
¹/₂	tsp Salt
¹/₂	tsp Soup Soy Sauce
¹/₂	Tbsp Sesame Seeds

AERI'S TIPS

• This uses hot peppers, but sweet peppers can be used instead to reduce the spiciness.

Method #1: Add all the ingredients in a large mixing bowl. Mix well until the sugar dissolves. Chill for several hours before serving.

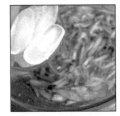

Method #2: For a faster method, substitute the 1¹/₂ cups of water with 1 cup of water and 1 cup of ice.

When the ice melts, it will change the balance of the salt, sugar, and vinegar. So, be careful about the amount of water in this recipe before you serve it.

This cold side is a very refreshing summer dish. It is delicious with both cooked rice and noodles. Cucumbers and cold water, seasoned with vinegar, sugar, and sesame seeds, tastes cool and delicious. You can add soaked dried seaweed (MiYeok or Wakame) also.

Tofu Buchim

Yield: 2 Servings

두부부침, DuBuBuChim

INGREDIENTS

1   Pack Firm Tofu (18 oz), 1 x $^1/_2$ Inch Pieces
     Some Green Onion, Minced (Garnish)

For the Sauce
2   Tbsp Hot Pepper Powder
$^1/_2$ Tbsp Garlic, Minced
$^1/_2$ Tbsp Sesame Oil
1   tsp Sesame Seeds
1   Tbsp Sugar
$2^1/_2$ Tbsp Soy Sauce

Rinse the firm tofu once, and wipe it with a paper towel gently. Firm tofu is the best to use for this dish.

Fry the tofu pieces until they become golden brown. Put the fried tofu on a plate, and pour some sauce on top, followed by some chopped green onions.

Combine the ingredients for the sauce. Mix everything together.

Add some oil in a nonstick preheated pan and then place the tofu pieces in it.

Beans are sometime called "the meat of the field," because they are a good source of protein. So, tofu is a very popular food in Korea. This dish is a little crispy on the outside, yet soft inside. The special sauce tastes great, and this will match well with a number of different foods. If you reduce the spiciness, it can be a good finger food for kids.

Spinach Jangtteok

시금치장떡, SiGeumChiJangTteok

Yield: $1^1/_2$ Dozen Pancakes

AERI'S TIPS

- I used $1^1/_2$ cups of all-purpose flour and $^1/_2$ cup of Korean frying mix instead of 2 cups of flour to get a more crispy texture. You can use just 2 cups of flour, but if you have the frying mix, I recommend that you use it.

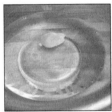

To make crispy pancakes, start by mixing the egg in the cold water.

Spread out a spoonful of the batter in a heated and generously oiled pan. Fry on medium-high until both sides become golden brown.

Add the flour, hot pepper paste, and salt to the egg and water. Mix everything together. Make sure that the hot pepper paste has completely dissolved.

Put the veggies into the batter. Mix.

Jangtteok is a food from eastern Korea. It is a little different from normal jeon. The main difference is the batter. It has soybean paste or hot pepper paste in it. You can add different kinds of veggies or meat in the batter too. This recipe uses hot pepper paste. They are very delicious and simple to make. It has enough flavor by itself that you don't need any dipping sauce.

Squid & Watercress Chomuchim

Yield: 2 Cups

오징어 미나리초무침, OJingEo MiNaRiChoMuChim

INGREDIENTS

1 Medium Squid (About $^2/_3$ Cup)	$^1/_2$ Tbsp Hot Pepper Powder
$3^1/_2$ oz Watercress, Washed, 3-Inch Lengths	4 tsp Brown Rice Vinegar or Apple Vinegar
$^1/_3$ Cup Onion, Thinly Sliced	1 Tbsp Sugar
$^1/_2$ Cup Cucumber, Diagonally Sliced	1 tsp Garlic, Minced
	1 tsp Sesame Seeds
For the Seasoning	1 tsp Sesame Oil
$2^1/_2$ Tbsp Hot Pepper Paste	$^1/_4$ tsp Salt

Make horizontal scratches in the squid with a knife to make a fancy pattern. The lines should be about $^1/_4$-inch apart. Be very careful to not press too hard or you will cut through the squid.

Divide the squid in half. Make scratches in the squid like before, but in the vertical direction and about $^1/_8$-inch apart. Every third scratch, cut all the way through. You will get about $^2/_3$ of a cup.

In boiling water, add the watercress and some salt. Boil it for about 20 seconds on high. The salt and the short boiling time help keep the watercress green.

Quickly put the boiled watercress in ice water. This is another tip for maintaining its nice green color.

In 2 cups of boiling water, add the squid. Cook for about 3 minutes on high. The boiled squid will have a nice pattern.

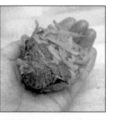

Squeeze the water out of the watercress. You will get about $^1/_3$ cup of watercress.

Combine the squid, watercress, onion, cucumber, and the seasoning ingredients.

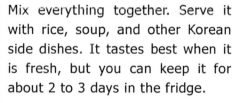

Mix everything together. Serve it with rice, soup, and other Korean side dishes. It tastes best when it is fresh, but you can keep it for about 2 to 3 days in the fridge.

Koreans like seafood a lot, so there are many different kinds of seafood dishes in Korean cuisine. This food is very common in Korea, especially in my hometown of Gwangju. The unique flavor of watercress is great in combination with the boiled squid and spicy sauce.

Fish Sausage Buchim

소세지부침, SoSeJiBuChim

Yield: 1¹/₂ Dozen Slices

INGREDIENTS

6   oz Korean Fish Sausage, ¹/₄-Inch Slices
¹/₈   Cup All-Purpose Flour
1   Egg, Beaten
1   Pinch Salt For Egg
       Vegetable Oil For Frying

 Break the egg and add 1 pinch of salt. Mix well.

 Spread out the flour on a plate. Cover the sausage with some flour.

 Dip the flour covered sausage into the egg mixture.

 Place the sausage pieces in a generously oiled and heated pan. Fry them on medium or medium-high.

 Fry until both sides of the sausage become golden brown.

This was one of the most popular lunch box sides during the good old days. When sausage was introduced in Korea, it was big hit. Then Koreans started to make fish sausage. Later, ham was introduced in Korea and it eventually replaced fish sausage in various foods. Slowly fish sausage became less popular. It is an old fashioned food now. Sometimes I miss this dish. It brings back my school day memories, and it still tastes good.

Spicy Fish Cake Bokkeum

Yield: 1 Quart

매운 어묵볶음, MaeUn EoMukBokkEum

1	Pack (14 oz) Fried Fish Cakes, $\frac{1}{2}$-Inch Strips
1	Cup Onion, $\frac{1}{4}$-Inch Slices
$\frac{1}{2}$	Cup Sweet Pepper, $\frac{1}{4}$-Inch Slices
$\frac{1}{3}$	Cup Carrot, Julienned
2	Tbsp Vegetable Oil

For the Sauce
2	Tbsp Soy Sauce
2	Tbsp Hot Pepper Powder
2	Tbsp Corn Syrup

2	Tbsp Cooking Wine (or Water)
1	tsp Sesame Oil
2	Pinches Black Pepper
1	tsp Garlic, Minced
1	tsp Sesame Seeds (Garnish)
	Salt to Taste

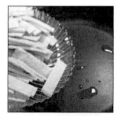

Heat 2 Tbsp olive oil in a pan. After the pan gets hot, fry the fish cakes for 3 minutes.

Set it aside.

Add the onion and cook for 2 more minutes.

Add and mix all the ingredients for the sauce in a big pan. Heat it until it boils, and then reduce to medium. Add the fried fish cakes and veggies to the sauce. Add salt to taste.

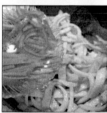

Cook the sweet pepper and carrot for 20 seconds.

Fry for 5 more minutes on medium and turn off the heat.

In the past, most Korean students brought their own lunch to school everyday because schools didn't have a cafeteria like they do nowadays. Spicy fish cake bokkeum was a common side dish for our lunch boxes, and because of that, it brings back memories of my school days. It is also a common side for homemade meals. If you like spicy food, you can add more hot pepper powder. Store this in the fridge and serve it with rice.

Cucumber Chojeolim

오이초절임, OIChoJeolIm

Yield: $^2/_3$ Cup

1	Cup Cucumber, Cut in Half Lengthwise, Diagonally Sliced
$^1/_2$	tsp Salt
2	tsp Sugar
2	tsp Vinegar

AERI'S TIPS

- Keep this in the refrigerator and use it whenever you serve your noodles.

In a bowl, add the cucumber and salt. Set it aside for about 15 minutes.

Mix together the salted cucumber, sugar, and vinegar.

Rinse the cucumber in cold water twice and drain.

This is a simple cucumber dish for garnishing mul naengmyeon or bibim naengmyeon, although you can use it as a side dish, or you can use it in other noodle dishes too. The sweet and sour flavor in this cucumber dish gives extra flavor to the main dish.

Korean Radish Chojeolim

Yield: 1 Cup

무초절임, MuChoJeolIm

INGREDIENTS

```
8    oz Korean Radish
1    tsp Salt
1    Tbsp Sugar
1    Tbsp Vinegar
1    tsp Hot Pepper Powder
```

AERI'S TIPS

- You can use a vegetable slicer or peeler to get these thin slices.

 Cut a Korean radish into about $\frac{1}{2}$-inch thick slices. Then slice the radish very thinly. Try to slice it as thin as you can, but thicker than paper.

 In a bowl, add the radish and 1 tsp of salt. Set it aside for about 30 minutes.

 Rinse the radish in cold water twice and drain.

 Mix the salted radish and the rest of the ingredients. Keep this in the fridge and use it whenever you serve your noodles.

This is a simple radish dish for garnishing mul naengmyeon or bibim naengmyeon, although you can use it as a side dish, or you can use it in other noodle dishes too. The sweet and sour flavor in this gives extra flavor to the main dish.

Spicy Chicken Galbi

닭갈비, DakGalBi

Yield: 2 Servings

INGREDIENTS

2	Green Onions, 1-Inch Pieces
$\frac{1}{2}$	Cup Onion, $\frac{1}{2}$-Inch Slices
$\frac{1}{2}$	Cup Cabbage, 1-Inch Pieces
$\frac{1}{2}$	Cup Sweet Potato
10	Rice Cakes
6	Sesame Leaves, Sliced & Stems Discarded
$\frac{1}{4}$	Cup Water
$\frac{1}{2}$	Tbsp Vegetable Oil
$\frac{1}{2}$	Tbsp Sesame Oil
	Sesame Seeds (Garnish)

For the Chicken
1	Chicken Breast (8 oz)
$\frac{1}{2}$	Tbsp Cooking Wine (or Water)

$\frac{1}{4}$	tsp Garlic, Minced
1	Pinch Black Pepper

For the Sauce
$1\frac{1}{2}$	Tbsp Hot Pepper Powder
2	Tbsp Hot Pepper Paste
2	tsp Curry Powder
2	tsp Garlic, Minced
$1\frac{1}{4}$	Tbsp Soy Sauce
$\frac{1}{2}$	Tbsp Sugar
$\frac{1}{8}$	tsp Black Pepper
1	Tbsp Cooking Wine (or Water)
$\frac{1}{4}$	tsp Ginger, Minced

Mix together all the ingredients for the chicken in a bowl. Set it aside while you are preparing the other ingredients.

Mix together all the ingredients for the sauce in a small bowl.

Mix 2 spoons of the sauce into the chicken. Slice half of a sweet potato; then cut the slices in half. Discard the cabbage stem; cut the leaves into 1-inch squares.

Add the olive oil and sesame oil into a heated pan. Then add the cabbage, sweet potatoes, onion, and rice cakes. Place the chicken on top. Pour the water over it, so that it does not become dry.

When it starts to boil, add all the leftover sauce into it. Fry until the chicken is almost cooked. Occasionally stir it while it cooks.

Add the green onions and sesame leaves. Fry until all the ingredients are cooked. Before serving, sprinkle some sesame seeds on top.

Many tourists seek out this stir-fried chicken dish, made famous by the city of Chuncheon. Sometimes it is called "Chuncheon dakgalbi." It is traditionally grilled on stoneware. Just before finishing off the chicken, the leftovers are fried with rice for an extra tasty treat.

Beef Bulgogi

Yield: 3 Servings

소고기 불고기, SoGoGi BulGoGi

INGREDIENTS

3	Cups Beef (Sirloin Recommended), Thinly Sliced		1¹/₂	Tbsp Garlic, Minced
1	Cup Onion, Thinly Sliced		1	Pinch Ginger Powder
¹/₂	Cup Carrot, ¹/₄-Inch Strips		1	Tbsp Sesame Seeds
			¹/₄	tsp Black Pepper
			1	Tbsp Sesame Oil

For the Sauce
6 Tbsp Soy Sauce
3 Tbsp Sugar
3 Tbsp Asian Pear Juice
3 Tbsp Cooking Wine (or Water)
3 Tbsp Green Onion, Minced

Cut the beef thinly. It is easier to cut if you partially freeze the meat for about 15 minutes before slicing it.

Combine and mix all the ingredients for the sauce in a small mixing bowl.

Combine the meat, veggies, and the sauce in a large bowl.

Cover it with plastic wrap or put it in a container with a lid. Store the container in the refrigerator for at least half a day to marinate.

Add the marinated beef in a preheated pan on medium-high.

Cook until the beef is well done.

Bulgogi is one of the most famous Korean foods. Many tourists visit Korea and try this delicious dish and love it. It not only has good flavor, but the way of eating this food is unique. We usually grill bulgogi at the table while we are eating our meal in a restaurant. Then we wrap bulgogi with lettuce, along with some soybean paste, garlic, onion, carrot, and/or cucumber. If you have a chance to visit Korea, try it. If you cannot, then try my recipe at home.

Beef Meatball Twigim

소고기완자튀김, SoGoGiWanJaTwiGim

Yield: 2 Dozen Meatballs

INGREDIENTS

14 oz (2 Cups) Ground Beef	$^1/_2$ Cup Korean Breadcrumbs
2 Tbsp Garlic, Minced	1 Egg, Beaten
$^1/_2$ tsp Salt	
1 tsp Cooking Wine (or Water)	
1 tsp Soy Sauce	
$^1/_4$ tsp Black Pepper	
$^1/_4$ Cup All-Purpose Flour	

AERI'S TIPS

- Drop a few breadcrumbs into the heated oil to check the oil's temperature. If the breadcrumbs float right after you drop them, the oil is hot enough to fry the meatballs.

Combine the beef, garlic, salt, cooking wine, soy sauce, and black pepper. Mix and set it aside for 10 minutes. Then take a spoonful of beef, and make a small ball.

Place the flour on a plate. Cover the meatballs with the flour.

Cover the meatballs with the egg.

Place the breadcrumbs on a plate. Cover the meatballs with breadcrumbs. Firmly cover them several times so they become crispier.

Add the meatballs into the hot oil.

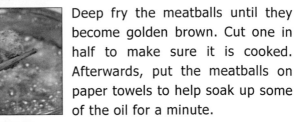

Deep fry the meatballs until they become golden brown. Cut one in half to make sure it is cooked. Afterwards, put the meatballs on paper towels to help soak up some of the oil for a minute.

This is another one of my mom's recipes. When I was young, my family lived in the peaceful country. In the morning, I would awaken to this awesome smell! I would sit next to her and enjoy watching her cook. My mom would make this for my father's lunch box and deliver it to him. My father loved this food. This was a good memory for me. We usually eat them just plain, but you can dip them in ketchup or honey mustard sauce too.

Stuffed Pepper Jeon

Yield: 3 Servings

고추전, GoChuJeon

INGREDIENTS

6	Hot Peppers, Seeded, Slit
1	Sweet Pepper, Seeded, $^1/_4$-Inch Slices
4	Eggs, Beaten (with 4 Pinches Salt)
$^1/_4$	Cup All-Purpose Flour

For the Meat

1	Cup Ground Beef or Pork

$1^1/_2$	Tbsp Green Onion, Finely Chopped
1	Tbsp Garlic, Minced
$1^1/_2$	Tbsp Soy Sauce
$^1/_2$	Tbsp Cooking Wine (or Water)
1	Tbsp Sugar
1	tsp Sesame Oil
$^1/_8$	tsp Black Pepper

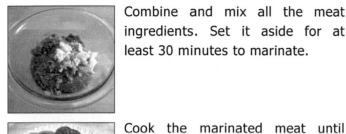

Combine and mix all the meat ingredients. Set it aside for at least 30 minutes to marinate.

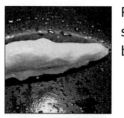

Roll the pepper and fry it until the surface of the stuffed pepper becomes golden brown.

Cook the marinated meat until completely cooked on medium. Cool the cooked meat. Then stuff it into the peppers.

Sprinkle some flour on both sides of the stuffed peppers. Spread some egg mixture in the pan in the shape of the sweet pepper. Place the pepper on top of the egg.

Cover the stuffed peppers with the flour.

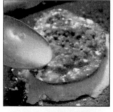

Spread some egg mixture across the top of the pepper.

Spread some egg mixture in a triangle shape. Place a stuffed pepper on the egg. Add more egg mixture to one side before you roll the pepper.

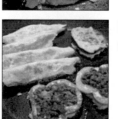

Fry until both sides of the pepper slices become golden brown.

Stuffed peppers in America are usually sweet peppers baked in the oven. Of course, they taste different from these Korean stuffed peppers, but the idea is similar. These are a common holiday food, and it is one of my favorite foods. I learned how to make them from my mom. We usually use less spicy peppers because you don't want the peppers to be overpowering. If you can't eat spicy food then use sweet peppers instead.

Spicy Chicken Bokkeumtang

닭볶음탕, DakBokkEumTang   Yield: 4 Servings

INGREDIENTS

2   Cups Onion, $^1/_2$-Inch Slices
2   Cups Potato, 1-Inch Cubes
1   Cup Carrot, 1-Inch Cubes
3   Green Onions, $^1/_2$-Inch Slices
1   Hot Pepper (Optional), $^1/_4$-Inch Slices
$1^1/_2$ Cups Water

For the Chicken
1   Whole Chicken (4 lb), 2-Inch Cubes
1   Tbsp Cooking Wine (or Water)
$^1/_4$ tsp Salt
$^1/_8$ tsp Black Pepper

For the Sauce
5   Tbsp Hot Pepper Paste
3   Tbsp Hot Pepper Powder
2   Tbsp Soy Sauce
$^1/_2$ Tbsp Cooking Wine (or Water)
1   Tbsp Sugar
1   Tbsp Corn Syrup
2   Tbsp Garlic, Minced
1   tsp Sesame Seeds
1   tsp Sesame Oil
1   Pinch Black Pepper

Mix together the chicken ingredients, and marinate it while you are preparing the other things.

Pour the sauce on top. Then pour the water over it.

Mix together all the ingredients for the sauce.

While it is cooking, occasionally stir it so that all the ingredients get covered with the sauce. Cook for 30 to 35 minutes on high, or until the chicken and potatoes are completely cooked.

Place the chicken in a big pan. Add the potatoes, onions, and carrots on top of the chicken.

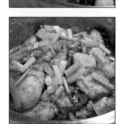
Reduce the temperature to low and add the green onions along with the hot peppers. Cook 2 more minutes, and then turn off the heat. If you don't want your food too spicy, skip the hot peppers.

Chicken and veggies cooked with a spicy sauce gives you great flavor in this dish. Depending on your tastes, you can adjust the amount of hot pepper powder and hot pepper paste. Serve this dish with rice and other Korean side dishes. You can also pour some of this on top of rice for a main course, in the same way as curry and rice.

Beef Tangsuyuk

Yield: 2 Servings

탕수육, TangSuYuk

INGREDIENTS

$^{1}/_{4}$ Cup Onion, $^{1}/_{2}$-Inch Slices	**For the Batter**
$^{1}/_{4}$ Cup Cucumber, $^{1}/_{2}$-Inch Slices	1 Cup Cornstarch
$^{1}/_{4}$ Cup Carrot, $^{1}/_{2}$-Inch Slices	$^{1}/_{2}$ Cup All-Purpose Flour
$^{1}/_{2}$ Cup Fruit Cocktail, Drained	1 Egg
	1 Cup Water

For the Beef

1 Cup Beef (Pork or Chicken), Thin Strips
3 Pinches Salt
3 Pinches Black Pepper
1 tsp Cooking Wine (or Water)

For the Sauce

$2^{1}/_{2}$ Tbsp Cornstarch
2 Tbsp Soy Sauce
4 Tbsp Sugar
4 Tbsp Brown Rice Vinegar or Apple Vinegar
1 Cup Water

 Mix together the beef ingredients. Set it aside for about 10 minutes to marinate.

 Fry the meat until the batter becomes lightly browned. You don't have to cook it completely in this step since it gets cooked again.

 Combine all the Ingredients for the batter. The consistency will be like crêpe batter.

 Fry the meat again until it becomes golden brown. Then, cool it on paper towels while you are preparing the sauce.

 Add the beef into the batter.

 Mix the sauce ingredients in a pan. Boil until it thickens. Add the fruit cocktail and chopped veggies. Boil for about 5 more minutes. Pour the sauce on the top of the fried beef, and serve.

Beef tangsuyuk is a Korean version of Chinese food. You can find this food in Chinese restaurants in Korea. (This is not authentic Chinese food.) The fried meat tastes really great with the sweet and sour sauce. The onions, carrots, and cucumbers give the sauce a wonderful combination of different flavors for the meat.

Beef Galbi

소갈비, SoGalBi

Yield: 3 Servings

INGREDIENTS

2¹/₂ lbs Beef Ribs (10 Pieces)
1 Cup (10 oz) Asian Pear, Chopped
¹/₂ Cup Onion, Chopped

1 Tbsp Sesame Oil
¹/₄ tsp Black Pepper
3 Tbsp Green Onions, Minced

For the Sauce
¹/₂ Cup Soup Soy Sauce
2 Tbsp Cooking Wine (or Water)
1¹/₂ Tbsp Garlic, Minced
1 tsp Ginger, Minced
1¹/₂ Tbsp Sugar
1¹/₂ Tbsp Honey

Soak the beef ribs in water for about 2 or 3 hours to get rid of the blood. Change the water every hour after some of the blood leaches out.

Then drain and rinse the ribs.

Grind the pear and onion together in a blender. Then mix that together with the ribs and set it aside for an hour. This will help reduce the strong meat flavor and make the meat sweet and tender.

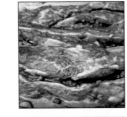

Combine all the ingredients for the sauce. Mix everything until the sugar and honey dissolves. Pour the sauce mixture on the beef ribs and mix again.

Cover the ribs with plastic wrap and marinate them for a day in the fridge. Flip over all the ribs once or twice while they are marinating.

The next day, grill some of the marinated beef ribs with a little of the extra sauce on a heated pan or grill. Cook them until the ribs are well done.

This recipe is for the very popular dish called "galbi," which is a type of BBQ. There are two main flavors. One is spicy and the other is sweet & salty. The latter type uses mainly soy sauce, pear, honey, sugar, apple, kiwi, etc. Many restaurants have indoor grills at each table so that customers can grill their own meat and enjoy the freshly cooked flavor. You can freeze some of the marinated meat to grill later.

White Fish Jeon

Yield: 16 Patties

흰 살 생선전, Huin Sal SaengSeonJeon

INGREDIENTS

12 oz Haddock or other White Fish, 1-Inch Cubes	1 Egg
1/4 Cup Carrot, 1-Inch Slices	1/2 Cup All-Purpose Flour
1/3 Cup Onion, 1-Inch Slices	1/2 tsp Salt
3 Garlic Cloves	1/8 tsp White Pepper Powder
1 1/2 Tbsp Green Onion, Finely Chopped	Vegetable Oil for Frying
1 tsp Hot Pepper, Finely Chopped	

AERI'S TIPS

• These fish cakes can be made with any kind of white fish such as haddock, halibut, or whiting fillet. I liked most of them, but halibut and haddock was the best. They are very delicious.

Grind the fish for few seconds (about 5), or until the fish becomes small pieces.

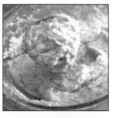

You will get a thick consistency like potato salad.

Add the onion, carrot, garlic, and about 3 Tbsp of water to the fish. Grind them for a minute, or until they become a paste.

Spread a spoonful of the fish mixture into a heated and oiled pan.

Combine the fish mixture, green onion, hot pepper, egg, flour, salt, and white pepper powder in a mixing bowl.

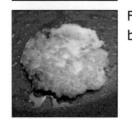

Fry them on medium-high, until both sides become golden brown.

These Korean style white fish cakes are really delicious. They make a perfect dish with a good mild fish flavor along with extra veggies and a little bit of flour. You can prepare the fish mixture ahead and fry it just before serving. In that point, it can be a good party food as an appetizer or side dish.

Sea Snail Muchim

골뱅이무침, GolBaengIMuChim   Yield: 3 Servings

INGREDIENTS

1	Cup/Can Sea Snails (GolBaengI), Drained, Washed
1	Cup Cucumber, Sliced
$1/2$	Cup Onion, Sliced
$1/3$	Cup Carrot, Sliced
1	Handful Cabbage or Romain Lettuce
3	Green Onions
1	Red Hot Pepper, $1/2$-Inch Slices
1	Green Hot Pepper, $1/2$-Inch Slices
5	Sesame Leaves (Optional)

For the Sauce

3	Tbsp Hot Pepper Paste
1	Tbsp Hot Pepper Powder
$1/2$	Tbsp Soy Sauce
2	Tbsp Sugar
2	Tbsp Vinegar
$1/8$	Tsp Garlic Powder
$1/2$	Tbsp Sesame Seeds

If the snails are too big, cut them into bite sized pieces.

Chop the cabbage (or Romain lettuce) into bite sized pieces. If you use cabbage, slice it into thin strips. Slice the perilla leaves like the cabbage.

Slice the green onions thinly, lengthwise.

In a small bowl, combine the sauce ingredients. Mix them all together. Start with 2 Tbsp of sugar and vinegar and add more, depending on your tastes.

In a large bowl, add all the sea snails and the prepared veggies.

Pour the sauce on the veggies and mix.

This is a popular dish that Korean people eat as a snack when they drink. Of course nondrinkers eat it too. You can get a can of sea snails in an Asian or Korean store. You can substitute them with boiled squid or shrimp. This dish is great with thin noodles. It is a little spicy, sweet, and sour. You can adjust the amount of sugar and vinegar to suit your tastes. It is best with just the right amount of sweet and sour flavor.

Beef Patty Galbi

Yield: 2 Dozen Patties

떡갈비, TteokGalBi

INGREDIENTS

1	lb Ground Beef
1	Cup Onion, Chopped
$1/_2$	Cup Carrot, Chopped
3	Green Onions, Minced
6	Garlic Cloves, Minced

For the Seasoning
4   Tbsp Soy Sauce

$1^1/_2$	Tbsp Sugar
2	Tbsp Honey
1	Tbsp Sesame Oil
$1/_2$	tsp Black Pepper
1	Tbsp Cooking Wine (or Water)
$1/_4$	tsp Salt (Optional)

AERI'S TIPS

- You may want to reduce the garlic or onion.
- This would be a good dish for a party or potluck meal.

Grind the veggies for few seconds in a food processor. We will grind them with the beef later, so they don't have to be ground that fine.

Slowly add some of the ground beef and grind until it becomes like dough.

Combine the meat mixture and all the seasoning ingredients in a mixing bowl. Kneed for about 2 minutes, this will help blend the various flavors, as well as develop a consistent texture.

Take a golf ball sized piece of the beef, make it round, and then flatten it. Place it in a slightly oiled nonstick pan. Fry on medium. It will burn if you cook it on high.

Once the juice comes out of the meat, flip it over and press it down with a spatula. Reduce to medium-low. Occasionally flip them over. Fry them until both sides become nicely browned.

If this recipe is too big, you can freeze some for later. Use wax paper to keep the patties separated in a freezer bag. Later, just get them out and fry - start on low, then increase to medium.

Tteok galbi is similar to galbi, which is a good representation of Korean food flavor. The texture is a little like sticky rice cakes, which is how it got its name, since "tteok" means sticky rice cakes in Korean. Oddly enough, there are no sticky rice cakes, or even rice flour, in this recipe. The soy sauce, sugar, garlic, green onion, and sesame oil makes this dish very flavorful. It tastes great.

Perilla & Beef Jeon

깻잎 고기전, GgaetIp GoGiJeon   Yield: 15 Leaves

INGREDIENTS

15	Perilla Leaves, Washed, Drained
2	Large Eggs
1/4	Cup All-Purpose Flour
	Vegetable Oil for Frying

For the Beef

1	Cup Ground Beef or Pork
1	tsp Cooking Wine (or Water)
1/8	tsp Salt
1/8	tsp Black Pepper

For the Filling

1/4	Cup Firm Tofu, Washed, Squeezed
1/4	Cup Onion, Finely Chopped
1	Large Egg
2	Tbsp Carrot, Finely Chopped
1 1/2	Tbsp Green Onion, Finely Chopped
1/2	Tbsp Garlic, Finely Chopped
1	Tbsp Soy Sauce
1/2	Tbsp Sesame Oil
1/8	tsp Black Pepper

 Mix all the beef ingredients together and marinate it for at least 10 minutes. Then add all the ingredients for the filling. Mix until everything sticks together nicely.

 Pour the flour on a flat plate. Evenly flour the backside of a perilla leaf. The flour helps the beef mixture stick to the perilla leaf.

 Spread about 1 Tbsp of beef mixture on one half of the floured side of the perilla leaf. About a 1/4-inch thickness of beef will be good.

 Fold the perilla leaf in half and cover the outer surface with flour.

 In a flat bowl, break 2 large eggs and whisk them gently. Mix in 2 pinches of salt. Dip both sides of the floured perilla leaf in the egg mixture.

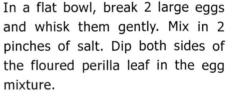 Fry them in a heated and liberally oiled pan. It is tricky to get the beef to cook completely without burning the perilla. With patience, fry each side for about 8 minutes on medium or medium-low.

Beef and perilla jeon is a creative way of cooking perilla leaves. I like food with a good match of flavors in the ingredients. This is a perfect example. The unique flavor of perilla tastes great with marinated beef. My husband loved this perilla jeon. He said that the raw perilla taste is gone; the jeon just tastes great. So, if you see perilla leaves in a Korean or Asian grocery store, please try this someday.

Oyster Jeon

Yield: 15 Pieces

굴전, GulJeon

INGREDIENTS

6	oz ($^3/_4$ Cup) Oyster
$^1/_4$	Cup All-Purpose Flour
1	Large Egg
2	Tbsp Green Onion, Minced
$^1/_2$	Tbsp Red Hot Pepper, Minced
4	Pinches Salt

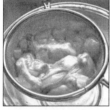
Wash the oysters in cold water and then drain.

Dip the floured oysters into the egg mixture.

Sprinkle two pinches of salt on the oysters and mix gently. Set aside while you are preparing the other ingredients.

Fry them in a heated and generously oiled pan on medium-high.

Combine one large egg, the chopped veggies, and 2 pinches of salt in a small mixing bowl.

When both sides become golden brown, they are done. You can serve them with soy dipping sauce.

Coat the salted oysters with the flour.

Oysters are popular and common in Korea. As a result, there are many different ways to eat them. This dish is one of them. Green onions and hot peppers are added for extra flavor. Since moving to the USA, I lost access to the many different kinds of fresh seafood that I enjoyed in Korea. One day we found a container of oysters in a nice grocery store. My eyes were sparkling with joy. They were not fresh enough to eat raw, but they were good enough for this.

Haddock Jeon

생선전, SaengSeonJeon

Yield: 3 Servings

12   oz. Haddock
$^1/_3$ Cup All-Purpose Flour
2   Eggs
Some Salt
Vegetable Oil for Frying

Slice the haddock into $^1/_4$-inch or thinner pieces. If the haddock is partially frozen, it is easier to cut.

Sprinkle some salt on each side of the sliced haddock evenly. If sized as in the picture, about 1 pinch of salt for each side will be enough. Set it aside for about 5 minutes.

Mix the eggs and 2 pinches of salt together.

Cover the salted haddock with flour.

Cover the floured haddock with the egg mixture. You can also add some finely chopped green onions into the egg mixture.

Add some oil (about 1 Tbsp) and place the battered haddock pieces into the pan.

Fry them until completely cooked and golden brown.

There are many types of jeon in Korean cuisine. Jeon is basically a fried food (made from meat, seafood, fish, veggies, etc.) that is covered with flour and eggs, or a batter. This recipe is a variety using fish. You can use any mild fish such as haddock or pollack; my favorite for this recipe is haddock. Since this is not deep fried, it will be healthier, and you will not lose the flavor with excessive grease. Koreans usually eat this as a side. It is best right after cooking it.

Beef Short Rib Jjim

Yield: 4 Servings

소갈비찜, SoGalBiJjim

INGREDIENTS

2	lb Beef Short Ribs, 1-Inch Cubes		1	Cup Onion, $1/2$-Inch Cubes
1	Cup Potato, $1/2$-Inch Cubes		6	Tbsp Soy Sauce
$1/2$	Cup Carrot, $1/2$-Inch Cubes		3	Tbsp Sugar
14	Peeled Chestnuts		3	Tbsp Cooking Wine (or Water)
$1^1/2$	Cups Beef Broth		2	Tbsp Green Onion, Finely Chopped
	Fried Egg (Garnish)		$1^1/2$	Tbsp Garlic, Minced
	Pine Nuts (Garnish)		1	Tbsp Sesame Oil
			$1/2$	Tbsp Sesame Seeds
For the Sauce			$1/4$	tsp Black Pepper
1	Cup Asian Pear, $1/2$-Inch Cubes		2	Pinches Ginger Powder

AERI'S TIPS

- The edges of the veggies will fall apart when cooking them. That will make your broth cloudy and thicker. To avoid that, cut off the edges of the veggie pieces with a vegetable peeler.

Soak the beef in cold water for at least an hour to draw out some of the blood. This will improve the flavor and texture.

An hour later, pour about 6 cups of water into a big pan and add the beef. Once it starts to boil, cook for 5 minutes on high. Take $1^1/2$ cups of beef broth from the pan and save it for later.

Drain the rest of the beef broth. Set aside the meat. This short boiling makes some broth; plus, cooked meat marinates better. Do this step twice to get rid of more fat if you want. I only did it once.

Blend the pear and onion to make a paste. (That is the secret for great flavor, and it helps tenderize the meat.) Then mix in all the sauce ingredients. Put the beef ribs into the sauce.

Marinate overnight in the fridge, or at least several hours. Boil the beef and the reserved broth. Once it's boiling, cook uncovered for an hour on medium-low. Boiling on high will make the meat tough.

Add the veggies and cook covered for 10 to 15 minutes on medium-high, or until the veggies soften. The broth will become very thick. Garnish with sesame seeds, pine nuts, and/or fried egg.

This is a popular traditional holiday or party food in Korea. Since it takes some time for the preparation, marination, and cooking, Koreans usually save this dish for special occasions. The meat is tender and delicious with a sweet and salty flavor to it.

Andong Jjimdak

안동 찜닭, AnDong JjimDak
Yield: 3 Servings

INGREDIENTS

2 lb Chicken
3 Cups Water
1¹/₂ oz Cellophane Noodles
1 Cup Potato, 1-Inch Cubes
1 Cup Onion, ¹/₂-Inch Pieces
¹/₂ Cup Carrot, ¹/₂-Inch Pieces
2 Green Onions, ¹/₂-Inch Pieces
1 Dried Red Hot Pepper, ¹/₂-Inch Pieces

3 Tbsp Cooking Wine (or Water)
3 Tbsp Dark Brown Sugar
1¹/₂ Tbsp Garlic, Minced
1¹/₂ tsp Sesame Oil
¹/₄ tsp Black Pepper
2 Pinches Ginger Powder

For the Sauce
4¹/₂ Tbsp Soy Sauce

Cook the chicken for a very short time (about a minute) in boiling water. This step helps to remove some of the fat and other things from the chicken.

Drain the fatty water and set the chicken aside.

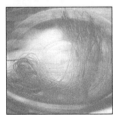

Soak the cellophane noodles in hot water while you are preparing the other ingredients.

Mix all the ingredients for the sauce. Place the chicken in a stockpot. Pour the sauce and 3 cups of water over the chicken. Once it starts to boil, reduce to medium and cook for 15 minutes.

Add the potato, onion, carrot, and dried pepper into the stockpot and cook for about 10 to 12 minutes on medium-high, or until all the ingredients are almost cooked.

Add the drained noodles and green onions. Cook for 3 more minutes, and then turn off the heat. Garnish with some sesame seeds.

Andong is the name of a Korean city, and this special dish is a very famous food from that area. It is also popular with many people that visit Korea. The braised chicken, veggies, and special sauce will make you fall in love with the flavor. There are some pre-made sauces for making this on the market. You can take a shortcut with one of those, but it is not too difficult to make from scratch.

Sweet & Spicy Tongdak

Yield: 2 Servings

양념 통닭, YangNyeom TongDak

INGREDIENTS

For the Chicken
2   lb Chicken (About $^1/_2$ Chicken)
$^1/_8$ Cup Milk
$^1/_4$ tsp Salt
$^1/_8$ tsp Black Pepper
1   Pinch Ginger Powder (Optional)

For the Batter
$^1/_4$ Cup Potato Starch or Cornstarch
$^1/_4$ Cup Frying Mix or All-Purpose Flour
$^1/_2$ Tbsp Korean Curry Powder
2   Pinches Salt
2   Pinches Black Pepper

For the Sauce *
$^1/_4$ Cup Ketchup
3   Tbsp Hot Pepper Paste
2   Tbsp Corn Syrup
1   Tbsp Sugar
1   Tbsp Onion, Minced
$^1/_2$ Tbsp Soy Sauce
$^1/_2$ Tbsp Garlic, Minced
$^1/_2$ Tbsp Vegetable Oil
1   Tbsp Sesame Seeds

* The sauce is only enough for half of the
  chicken. Double it if you want more.

Combine all the ingredients for the chicken. Marinate it for about 10 minutes. This step (especially the milk) helps to reduce some of the bad chicken flavor.

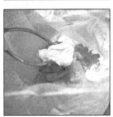

Add all the batter ingredients in a bag. Shake the bag to mix everything together. Then add all the chicken in the bag and shake. Shake until the chicken becomes evenly covered.

Take out the chicken and set it aside. Save the leftover flour mixture. Pour oil into a deep frying pan and heat it on high. When the oil becomes hot, the chicken will have become soggy.

Drop a little piece of the flour mixture into the oil. If it floats immediately, the oil is hot enough. Re-flour each piece of chicken right before frying it. Carefully put it into the oil.

Fry for 8-10 minutes, or until lightly browned. Remove and drain the chicken on a paper towel. Fry again for 5 minutes, or until golden brown. Make sure that the chicken has completely cooked.

Mix and cook all the sauce ingredients, sans sesame seeds. Once it starts to bubble, cook for 1 more minute. Coat half of the chicken with sauce. Garnish with sesame seeds.

This must be the most popular snack food in Korea. Many restaurants offer free delivery in Korea, until around midnight. Whenever people have to be up late into the night watching the Olympics, World Cup, etc., the fried chicken restaurants are very busy. This has a slightly sweet and spicy sauce. As a shortcut, you can make the sauce and buy KFC chicken. It is delicious plain or seasoned. Serve it with pickled radish and/or sweet corn salad.

Cheese Oven Spaghetti

치즈 오븐 스파게티, ChiJeu OBeun SeuPaGeTi

Yield: 3 Servings

INGREDIENTS

7   oz (1 Handful) Spaghetti
$^1/_2$ lb (1 Cup) Ground Beef
1   Cup Onion, Finely Diced
$^1/_2$ Cup Carrot, Finely Diced
2   Cups Mozzarella Cheese
1   Jar (15 oz) Spaghetti Sauce
$^1/_2$ Tbsp Garlic, Minced
$^1/_2$ tsp Black Pepper
       Salt
       Olive Oil
       Parsley (Garnish)

Fry the garlic, onion, and $^1/_2$ Tbsp olive oil for 10 seconds on high in a preheated pan. Add the beef, black pepper, and $^1/_2$ tsp salt. Brown the beef on medium high.

Add the onion and carrot. Cook for 3 minutes on high. In a pot of boiling water, add 1 handful of spaghetti, $^1/_2$ Tbsp of olive oil, and $^1/_2$ tsp of sea salt. Cook the spaghetti until it is almost done.

Drain the water from the spaghetti and add the cooked spaghetti to the meat. Stir gently. Add $1^1/_2$ Tbsp of olive oil and fry for 3 minutes on high.

In a dish safe for baking, place some mozzarella cheese across the bottom. Spread some spaghetti sauce on top of the cheese. Then add some spaghetti and meat on top of the sauce.

Spread some more sauce on top of the spaghetti. Sprinkle some cheese on top. Garnish with parsley flakes.

Bake it in a 425°F oven for about 10 minutes. Once the cheese starts to melt, change the oven to broil mode and bake it until the cheese becomes golden brown.

In Korea, cheese oven spaghetti is popular in pizza or other Western-style restaurants. This is my own version of cheese oven spaghetti. It is really good with its melted mozzarella cheese, meat, and veggies.

Curry Bap

Yield: 2 Servings

카레라이스, KaReRaISeu

| INGREDIENTS |

$^1/_2$ Cup Chicken Breast, Cubed	**For the Curry Paste**
3 Tbsp Peas	5 Tbsp Korean Curry Powder
1 Cup Potato, $^1/_2$-Inch Cubes	1 Tbsp Water
1 Cup Onion, $^1/_2$-Inch Cubes	
$^1/_2$ Cup Carrot, $^1/_2$-Inch Cubes	
2 Cups Water	

Fry the potatoes, with a pinch of salt, until they are almost completely cooked.

Add the fried veggies and meat in a large pot. Add the 2 cups of water and boil on high.

Fry the onions, with a pinch of salt, until they are almost completely cooked.

Once it starts to boil, add the peas, and cook for about 5-10 minutes, or until the potato has completely cooked.

Fry the carrots, with a pinch of salt, until they are almost completely cooked.

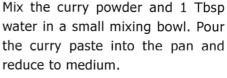

Mix the curry powder and 1 Tbsp water in a small mixing bowl. Pour the curry paste into the pan and reduce to medium.

Fry the chicken, with a little bit of salt and black pepper, until it is completely cooked.

Cook for about for 5 more minutes and then turn off the heat. Serve the curry on top of cooked rice. It is very good with any kind of kimchi.

Curry powder is considered to be very healthy. When I tried the common curry powder sold in American, I thought it tasted a little different compared to Korean curry. So, I used "Ottogi Curry Medium." That brand comes in three different heat levels: hot, medium, and mild. I usually use medium, but you can use whatever you want. This curry tastes best with chicken, rather than other meat. You can also skip the meat and it will still taste very good.

Spicy Cold Buckwheat Myeon

비빔냉면, BiBimNaengMyeon

Yield: 4 Cups Sauce

INGREDIENTS

	Buckwheat Noodles for NaengMyun		6	Garlic Cloves
	Some Cooked Beef, Thinly Sliced (2 Pieces for each Serving)		1	Green Onion, Chopped
			1	Hot Pepper, Chopped
	Hard Boiled Eggs, Halved (Half an Egg for Each Serving)		$1/_3$	Cup Hot Pepper Powder
			2	Tbsp Hot Pepper Paste
1	Asian Pear, Sliced (3 Slices for Each Serving)		3	Tbsp Brown Sugar
	Some Pickled Radish		3	Tbsp Honey
	Some Pickled Cucumber, Sliced (4 Pieces per Serving)		1	tsp Salt
			$1/_2$	Cup Crushed Pineapple
1	Tbsp Sesame Seeds		$1/_8$	Cup Korean Cider or Ginger Ale
			$1/_4$	Cup Vinegar
For the Sauce			2	Tbsp Soy Sauce
$1/_2$	Cup Asian Pear, Chopped		3	Tbsp Sesame Oil
$1/_4$	Cup Onion, Chopped		1	Tbsp Cooking Wine (or Water)

Add the ingredients for the sauce in a mixer. Grind everything together until it become smooth and fine.

Pour the sauce into a glass container. Combine and mix the sesame seeds. Keep the sauce in the fridge for at least a day or two before serving. That will help the flavors combine.

When the broth and toppings are ready, cook the needed amount of buckwheat noodles in boiling water for about 2 minutes. Follow the instructions from the noodle package that you have.

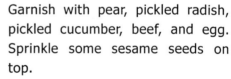

Drain and then rinse the cooked noodles in cold water twice.

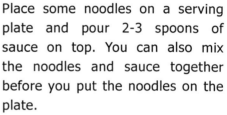

Place some noodles on a serving plate and pour 2-3 spoons of sauce on top. You can also mix the noodles and sauce together before you put the noodles on the plate.

Garnish with pear, pickled radish, pickled cucumber, beef, and egg. Sprinkle some sesame seeds on top.

In Korea, this dish is as popular as the cold buckwheat noodle soup "mul naengmyeon." "Bibim" means mixing something, "naeng" means cold, and "myeon" means noodle. We use the same toppings as mul naengmyeon: pickled radish, pickled cucumber, meat, hard-boiled egg, and Asian pear. You can freeze the sauce and use it later. Vegetarians can skip the beef. You can also substitute an apple for the Asian pear if you cannot find Asian pears.

Kimchi Ramyeon

Yield: 1 Serving

김치라면, GimChiRaMyeon

INGREDIENTS

1	Pack Korean Instant Noodles (Shin RaMyun)
3	Cups Water
$^1/_4$	Cup Kimchi, Bite-Sized Pieces
1	Egg
1	Green Onion, Finely Chopped
	Dried Seaweed to Garnish, Thinly Shredded

AERI'S TIPS

- You can use most kinds of Korean instant noodles for this recipe, but if you like spicy food, I recommend Shin Ramyun from the Nongsim company.

Boil 3 cups of water. Normally we need $2^1/_2$ cups of water to cook one pack of ramyun. However, since you will add some kimchi, you need more water for this recipe.

Add the noodles and cook for 3 more minutes. Stir it occasionally.

Add the kimchi to the boiling water.

Add one egg and cook for $2^1/_2$ minutes. Don't stir, because you don't want to have a strong egg flavor in your ramyun. When the egg white has cooked, break the yoke.

Then add the spice packets and cook for 1 minute. In this way, you will get more flavor from the kimchi.

Add the chopped green onion when 15 seconds are left. Save a few green onion pieces to garnish. Garnish with the green onion and seaweed.

Kimchi Ramyeon is one way to cook delicious Korean instant noodles. There are many different kinds of Korean instant noodles in the Korean or Asian store. Most Korean instant noodles have more flavor and are spicier than American instant noodles. Adding kimchi gives even more flavor and makes it spicier.

Kimchi Bokkeumbap

김치볶음밥, GimChiBokkEumBap   Yield: 2 Servings

INGREDIENTS

1	Cup Kimchi, Bite-Sized Pieces
2	tsp Sugar
$1/_2$	tsp Salt
1	Tbsp Vegetable Oil
2	Tbsp Kimchi Liquid
$1/_2$	tsp Sesame Oil
2	Eggs

Some Sesame Seeds (Garnish)
2   Cups Short Grain Rice, Cooked

AERI'S TIPS

- You can also fry the eggs in the rice. To do so, break the eggs in a bowl and mix them together. Pour the egg into the fried rice and stir.
- "Kimchi liquid" is the liquid that forms while the kimchi is fermenting.

 Add some oil in a heated pan and fry the kimchi. Add the sugar. Fry for about 5 minutes on medium-high.

 Fry the eggs. Add salt to taste. When they are done, place them on a plate, and put the rice on top of the eggs.

 Add the cooked rice and salt.

 Add the kimchi liquid and fry 10 more minutes. Then add the sesame oil and fry for two more minutes.

There are a couple secrets to making delicious fried kimchi rice. First, good kimchi makes delicious fried kimchi rice. Well-fermented kimchi is the best. Another thing is: fry the kimchi first - don't cheat. I prefer to fry my rice so that it becomes crispy, which takes longer to cook. You can add more sugar or salt depending on your tastes.

Spicy Seafood Guksu

Yield: 3 Servings

짬뽕, JjamBbong

INGREDIENTS

12 Jumbo Shrimp (or 15 Small), Shelled
2/3 Cup Squid, Bite-Sized Pieces
15 Mussels, Washed
2/3 Cup Cabbage, Bite-Sized Pieces
1 Cup Onion, Bite-Sized Pieces
1/3 Cup Carrot, Bite-Sized Pieces
1 Handful Spinach, Bite-Sized Pieces
9 Stone Ear Mushrooms (SeogI BeoSeot), Bite-Sized Pieces
2 Hot Peppers (1 Red & 1 Green), 1/4-Inch Slices
1 Green Onion, 1/2-Inch Slices
  Thick Noodles for JjamBbong (Fresh or Frozen)

For the Broth
6 1/2 Cups Water
1 Dried Anchovy Pack (or 7 Dried Anchovies)
8 Pieces Dried Kelp (2 x 2 Inch)

For the Seasoning
4 Tbsp Hot Pepper Oil
1/2 Tbsp Garlic, Minced
2 Tbsp Cooking Wine (or Water)
3 Tbsp Hot Pepper Powder
4 Tbsp Soup Soy Sauce
2 Pinches of Black Pepper
  A Little Salt (Optional)

Boil the broth ingredients for 5 minutes on medium. Then remove the kelp from the broth. Boil 10 more minutes, and then remove the anchovy pack. You should get about 6 cups of broth.

In a heated pan, fry the hot pepper oil and minced garlic together for 10 seconds on high. Then pour the broth into the pan and add the cabbage, onion, and carrot.

Add the rest of the seasonings. Boil for about 7 minutes on medium high. While the soup is boiling, start boiling the water for the noodles.

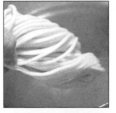
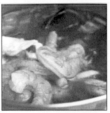

Once the water starts to boil, add the noodles and cook for about 7 minutes. (If you have instructions for your noodles follow them instead.)

Add the seafood. Once, it starts to boil again, add the mushrooms and spinach. (If you have dried mushrooms, soak them in water to soften them before cutting.) Boil for 5 more minutes on high.

Add the green onions and peppers. Cook for 1 more minute. Rinse the noodles in cold water several times. To serve, place some noodles in a bowl and then pour the soup on top.

Jjambbong is a Korean version of spicy Chinese seafood noodles. It is as popular as jajangmyun (blackbean paste noodles) in Korea. You need many ingredients to make this, but it is not that difficult to make, and it does not take a long time. The great flavor from the spicy seafood broth and thick noodles can be the ideal dish for the spicy seafood lover. Homemade broth from fresh ingredients is much better then semi-artificial flavorings like MSG.

Beef Kimbap

소고기 김밥, SoGoGi GimBap

Yield: 10 Rolls

INGREDIENTS

10	Sheets Dried Seaweed		1	Tbsp Sugar
9	oz Spinach ($^1/_2$ Cup Boiled Spinach)		$^1/_2$	Tbsp Cooking Wine (or Water)
20	Strips Burdock Root, $^1/_4$-Inch, Seasoned		1	tsp Sesame Oil
10	Strips Pickled Radish, $^1/_4$-Inch (DanMuJi)		$^1/_8$	tsp Black Pepper
1	Cup Carrot, Julienned, Fried			
5	Eggs			**For the Rice**
			$7^1/_2$	Cups Short Grain Rice, Cooked
	For the Beef		1	tsp Salt
$^1/_2$	lb (1 Cup) Ground Beef		$1^1/_2$	Tbsp Sesame Oil
1	Green Onion, Finely Chopped		$1^1/_2$	Tbsp Vegetable Oil
1	Tbsp Garlic, Minced		$^1/_2$	Tbsp Sesame Seeds
$1^1/_2$	Tbsp Soy Sauce			

Mix together the ingredients for the beef. Set it aside while you are preparing the other ingredients. After it finishes marinating, fry it until it has completely cooked.

Boil the spinach with some salt (to help retain the color) for 30 seconds. Then rinse in cold water and squeeze out the water. Mix together the spinach, $^1/_2$ tsp of sesame oil, and 2 pinches of salt.

Break 5 eggs. Mix in 5 pinches of salt. Oil a pan and cook them on medium until they are almost done. Reduce to low and flip them over. Fry them until both sides of are done. Cut into $^1/_2$-inch strips.

In a large bowl, mix together the rice ingredients. Mix gently, so that your rice will not get mushy. Cover your rice with plastic wrap so that it does not dry out.

Place the shiny side of a dried seaweed sheet face down on a bamboo mat. Spread rice across $^2/_3$ of the seaweed, and on top of that, the burdock, egg, carrot, spinach, beef, and pickled radish.

Roll it tightly. Put some rice on the end of the seaweed sheet to help seal it. Roll it with the bamboo mat and squeeze it hard (important for good shape). Coat it with sesame oil and then slice it.

Beef kimbap is a type of Korean kimbap. Green, orange, yellow, black, white, brown - the color combination from the ingredients are very good. Of course, the taste is even better. I used the same recipe for the beef here as the beef in my Korean stuffed pepper recipe.

Cold Buckwheat Guksu

Yield: 4 Servings

물냉면, MulNaengMyeon

INGREDIENTS

4	Servings Buckwheat Noodles for NaengMyeon
2	Hard Boiled Eggs, Halved
1	Cup Asian Pear, Sliced
	Some Pickled Radish
	Some Pickled Cucumber
	Some Sesame Seeds
2	tsp Soup Soy Sauce
1	tsp Salt
1	Tbsp Sugar
$1^1/_2$	Tbsp Vinegar

For the Broth

10	oz Beef
4	oz Korean Radish
12	Cups Water
$^1/_2$	Cup Onion
2	Green Onions
6	Garlic Cloves
1	Fingernail Sized Piece of Ginger
5	Pieces Kelp (1 x 2 Inch)
$^1/_2$	tsp Peppercorns

Boil all the broth ingredients and the beef for five minutes. Then remove the kelp and cook for $1^1/_2$ hours on medium. Occasionally remove the foam from the surface of the broth.

After the broth is done, drain the broth with cheesecloth to make the broth clear. Only save the broth and the beef; discard the rest. You will get about 5 cups of beef broth.

Mix together the soy sauce, salt, sugar, and vinegar. You may want to adjust the vinegar, sugar, or salt. Store this in the fridge, and place it in the freezer for about 3 hours before serving.

When the beef has cooled down, slice it thinly to use as a topping later. Boil the buckwheat noodles for about 2 minutes. Drain and then rinse the cooked noodles in cold water twice.

In a serving bowl, add some noodles and garnish with the pickled radish, pear, pickled cucumber, beef, and egg.

Take the broth out of the freezer. It should be a little icy. Pour some broth in the bowl right before serving. That way the ice will not melt away before eating. Garnish with some sesame seeds.

Cold buckwheat noodle soup is a favorite summer dish in Korea. It is a very cool and refreshing meal. You can make a large portion of broth and beef and freeze it for later. That way, you can quickly and easily prepare this dish. It can be a little complex and time consuming to make, but it is worth the effort. Depending on your tastes, you can add a little bit of Korean mustard paste or vinegar.

Soybean Sprout Bap

콩나물밥, KongNaMulBap

Yield: 6 Servings

INGREDIENTS

1   lb (6 Cups) Soybean Sprouts, Washed Twice and Removed Bad Parts
2   Cups Short Grain Rice
1   Piece Dried Kelp (3 x 2 Inch)

For the Beef
$^1/_2$ lb (1 Cup) Ground Beef
1   Tbsp Soy Sauce
1   Tbsp Green Onion, Finely Chopped
$^1/_2$ Tbsp Cooking Wine (or Water)
$^1/_2$ Tbsp Garlic, Minced

1   tsp Sesame Oil
2   Pinches Black Pepper

For the Sauce
4   Tbsp Soy Sauce
2   Tbsp Green Onion, Minced
1   Tbsp Garlic, Minced
1   Tbsp Hot Pepper Powder
$^1/_2$ Tbsp Sugar
$^1/_2$ Tbsp Sesame Oil
$^1/_2$ Tbsp Sesame Seeds

Wash one cup of short grain rice at least twice in cold water. You can soak the rice in water for about 10 minutes to get better texture. Drain.

Put the kelp on top of the rice. Pour some water on top. Add a slightly smaller amount of water than you normally would (the bean sprouts will add some liquid as they cook).

Combine and mix all the ingredients for the beef. Place the marinated beef on top of the rice and kelp. Spread the beef evenly so it will cook better.

Add the soybean sprouts on top of everything and cook it with the "white rice" setting. It will take about 45 minutes to an hour depending on your rice cooker.

Once the rice is done cooking, remove the kelp from the rice cooker and throw it away. Move the cooked rice and bean sprouts to a bigger bowl to mix.

Stir everything gently. Break any large chunks of beef into smaller pieces. Mix all the ingredients for the sauce together. To serve: place some in a bowl and top with sauce. Mix together before eating.

Soybean sprout bap is a delicious and unique one dish meal. When you make the rice, you cook some marinated meat and bean sprouts together, and then eat it with a special sauce. For this recipe, I used my rice cooker; however, you can also cook the rice on the stove.

Kimchi Bibimguksu

Yield: 2 Servings

김치 비빔국수, GimChi BiBimGukSu

INGREDIENTS

5¹/₂ oz Thin Noodles (About 2 Cups Cooked)
1 Cup Well Fermented Kimchi, Bite Sized Pieces

For the Sauce
1 Tbsp Soy Sauce
¹/₂ Tbsp Green Onion, Finely Chopped

1 tsp Hot Pepper Powder
1 tsp Sesame Oil
¹/₂ tsp Sesame Seeds
¹/₂ tsp Garlic, Minced
¹/₄ tsp Sugar

AERI'S TIPS

- I like Sempio's thin noodles for this recipe because of their good flavor and nice texture, so I highly recommend them. If you don't have them, try angel hair spaghetti instead.

Cook the thin noodles in boiling water on medium-high for 3 to 5 minutes.

Once the noodles are done cooking, immediately drain and then them rinse in cold water several times to improve the texture.

Combine all the ingredients for the sauce.

Add the noodles, the sauce, and the kimchi into a large mixing bowl.

It is important to use good tasting and well fermented kimchi for this dish.

Mix everything gently; it is ready to serve.

This is a slightly spicy noodle dish with kimchi that is served cold. It can be good for any time of year, but it is especially good for your lunch during a hot summer day because it only takes few minutes to make, and the noodles are cool. Well-fermented kimchi, along with the thin noodles and special sauce, tastes great.

Oyster Juk

굴죽, GulJuk

Yield: 3 Servings

INGREDIENTS

10	oz (1 Cup) Fresh Oysters, Rinsed
1	Cup Short Grain Rice (Or Glutinous Rice)
5	Cups Water
2	Pieces Dried Kelp (3 x 4 Inch)
$^1/_2$	Cup Oyster Mushrooms, Finely Chopped
$^1/_4$	Cup Green Onion, Finely Chopped
2	Tbsp Carrot, Finely Chopped

$1^1/_2$	Tbsp Sesame Oil
$^1/_2$	tsp Salt
	Grilled Laver (Garnish)
	Sesame Seeds (Garnish)

Wash and then soak the rice in water for about 30 minutes.

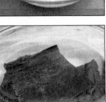

At the same time, soak the dried kelp in 5 cups of cold water for about 30 minutes. This will make good broth. If you do not have kelp, just using normal water for your porridge.

In a heated pan, fry the soaked and drained rice with the sesame oil. Fry for 2 minutes on high. Keep stirring so that the rice will not stick to the bottom of the pan.

Pour the 5 cups of kelp broth (or water) into the rice. Once it starts to boil, cook for 15 minutes on medium, or until the rice has almost finished cooking. Stir it occasionally.

Add the oysters, mushroom, and carrot. Cook for three more minutes on high.

Add the chopped green onions and cook for another minute. Then turn off the heat.

Add salt to taste.

Oyster juk is very popular in the winter because that is the best season for good oysters. This is one of the many different kinds of porridge in Korean cuisine. For some good variations to this recipe, simply replace the oysters with some other seafood such as: clams, mussels, shrimp, scallops, etc. You can also substitute your favorite mushroom. I used only the tops of the green onions for better color.

Beef Jumeokbap

Yield: 45 Rice Balls

소고기 주먹밥, SoGoGi JuMeokBap

INGREDIENTS

2¹/₂ Cups Short Grain Rice, Cooked
¹/₃ Cup Zucchini, Finely Chopped
¹/₃ Cup Potato, Finely Chopped
¹/₃ Cup Onion, Finely Chopped
¹/₄ Cup Sweet Peppers, Finely Chopped
¹/₈ Cup Carrot, Finely Chopped
Some Seasoned Dried Laver (Optional)

For the Beef
7 oz (³/₄ Cup) Ground Beef
1 Tbsp Soy Sauce

1 Tbsp Dark Brown Sugar
1 Tbsp Garlic, Minced
1 Tbsp Green Onion, Finely Chopped
1 tsp Sesame Oil
¹/₈ tsp Black Pepper

For the Seasoning
¹/₂ Tbsp Sesame Seeds
1 tsp Sesame Oil
¹/₄ tsp Salt

 Combine and mix all the ingredients for the beef. Let it marinate while you are preparing the other ingredients.

 In a heated pan, brown the marinated beef.

 Add the chopped veggies and fry for about 5 minutes on medium-high. Finely chopped veggies will make it easier to make the rice balls later. You can add a little bit of cooking oil if needed.

 Gently mix it into the cooked rice. Mix in the seasoning ingredients. You may want to add salt. If you are going to use seasoned seaweed, use less salt in this step.

 Make a round ball with a spoonful of rice. Try to make the balls firm so that they will stick together. When you make them, it will be easier if your hands are covered with a little bit of water or oil.

 To make seaweed rice balls, place several pieces of seasoned dried seaweed inside of a plastic bag. Break them into little pieces with your hands. Roll the rice balls in the bag to cover the balls.

Jumeokbap is literally translated as "fist rice" because it looks like a fist. People had to prepare simple and easy meals for the soldiers in the Korean war, and this food was great in that point. Also, this can be easily taken anywhere. Later, it became popular for packed lunches at work and school. Nowadays, there are a variety of flavors such as kimchi, seafood, tuna, etc. Also, the size has became smaller and it has become more colorful and flavorful.

Veggie Bokkeumbap

야채볶음밥, YaChaeBokkEumBap

Yield: 2 Servings

INGREDIENTS

2	Cups Short Grain Rice, Cooked
$^2/_3$	Cup Potato, Finely Chopped
$^2/_3$	Cup Onion, Finely Chopped
$^1/_3$	Cup Carrot, Finely Chopped
$^1/_3$	Cup Sweet Pepper, Finely Chopped
$^2/_3$	Cup Zucchini, Finely Chopped
2	Eggs (+2 Pinches Salt)

$^1/_2$	tsp Salt
	Vegetable Oil for Frying
	Sesame Seeds (Garnish)

 Heat 2 Tbsp of oil in a pan. Add the potato and onion into the heated pan. Fry them until the potatoes are half cooked.

 Push the rice to one side of the pan to make room to cook the eggs. Pour the egg mixture in the pan.

 Add the carrots, zucchini, and sweet pepper. Add $^1/_4$ tsp of salt and fry until the veggies are almost done cooking.

 Make scrambled eggs.

Add the rice and fry for 5 more minutes.

 When the eggs are almost cooked, mix them with the fried rice and cook for 2 more minutes.

 Meanwhile, break the eggs and add 2 pinches of salt. Beat the eggs.

Add $^1/_4$ tsp of salt. You may want to adjust the salt. It is done. As an option, you can add some sesame oil. Garnish with some sesame seeds.

Fried rice is very common in Asia. Depending on the country, the ingredients can vary somewhat. This recipe is one way to make a Korean-styled version. This is a very good way to use your old rice without wasting it. It is also a good way to get kids to eat their veggies. There are no particular rules for the ingredients. So, use whatever you have available. Ham, sausage, or hot dogs, makes it even more delicious. (Reduce the salt in those cases.)

Tuna Mayo Triangle Kimbap

Yield: 5 Servings   참치마요 삼각김밥, ChamChiMaYo SamGakGimBap

INGREDIENTS

5 Sheets Dried Laver (From Kit)	$^1/_4$ tsp Salt
$^1/_2$ Cup Tuna in Oil, Drained	1 tsp Sesame Oil
2 Tbsp Mayonnaise	1 tsp Sesame Seeds
1 Pinch Black Pepper	

For the Rice
$2^1/_2$ Cups Short Grain Rice, Cooked

Combine and gently mix the rice ingredients.

Combine the tuna, mayonnaise, and a pinch of black pepper. Mix everything together. You may want to add more mayonnaise or salt.

Place the side marked with the number "1" facedown, with the "1" at the top. Then place the plastic forming tool at the top. Evenly fill $^1/_3$ of the triangle shape with about $^1/_4$ cup of rice.

Add some of the filling on top of the rice. Leave about $^1/_8$-inch all around the filling; do not let the filling touch the forming tool. This helps prevent a mess later when we press it.

Getting the right amount of rice and filling is the key to getting the perfect taste and shape. Add another $^1/_4$ cup of rice on top of the filling.

Press the rice with the other plastic piece in the kit. Push it down to the line on the first plastic piece. Remove the plastic forming tools.

Fold the seaweed sheet up over the rice. Fold both sides of the seaweed down over the rice, and tuck the extra seaweed under the rice.

Fold both sides of the bottom seaweed piece up over the sides to the center of the triangle. Fasten each side with a piece of the tape.

Triangle kimbap is a very popular food sold in convenience stores in Korea. Since this kimbap is wrapped in a disposable plastic package, it is easy to carry and eat wherever or whenever you want. There are many different types available. This one uses tuna and mayo. You can find the kit for making this triangle kimbap in a Korean grocery store.

Beef Deopbap

소고기덮밥, SoGoGiDeopBap   Yield: 3 Servings

INGREDIENTS

3 Cups Short Grain Rice, Cooked	$^1/_2$ Tbsp Sugar
$^1/_2$ Cup Onion, Bite-Sized Pieces	$^1/_2$ Tbsp Sesame Oil
$^2/_3$ Cup Zucchini, Bite-Sized Pieces	3 Pinches Black Pepper
$^1/_2$ Cup Carrot, Bite-Sized Pieces	1 Pinch Ginger Powder
2 Green Onions, Bite-Sized Pieces	**For the Sauce**
3 Button Mushrooms, Bite-Sized Pieces	$^2/_3$ Tbsp Soy Sauce
$^1/_2$ Cup Sweet Peppers, Bite-Sized Pieces	1 tsp Sugar
1 Hot Pepper, Thinly Sliced (Optional)	2 Tbsp Vegetable Oil
	$^1/_2$ Tbsp Sesame Oil
For the Beef	1 tsp Sesame Seeds
10.5 oz Beef (London Broil), Thinly Sliced	$1^1/_2$ tsp Garlic, Minced
$^1/_4$ Cup Onion, Diced	$^1/_4$ tsp Salt
$^1/_2$ Cup Asian Pear, Diced	3 Pinches Black Pepper
1 Tbsp Cooking Wine (or Water)	**For the Starch**
3 Garlic Cloves	$^1/_2$ Cup Water
$2^1/_2$ Tbsp Soy Sauce	1 Tbsp Cornstarch or Potato Starch

In a mixer, add the beef ingredients, minus the beef. Grind them together. Pour the mixture into the beef.

Mix the beef and sauce together. Cover it with plastic wrap and let it marinate in the refrigerator for at least 2 hours.

Add 2 Tbsp of oil in a preheated pan. Add $1^1/_2$ tsp of minced garlic. Fry for 10 second on medium. Add the onion, carrot, zucchini, and sweet peppers. Fry for 1 to 2 more minutes on medium-high.

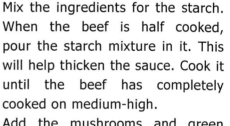
Add the marinated beef and the rest of the ingredients for the sauce.

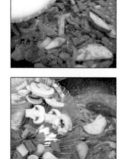
Mix the ingredients for the starch. When the beef is half cooked, pour the starch mixture in it. This will help thicken the sauce. Cook it until the beef has completely cooked on medium-high.

Add the mushrooms and green onions. If you like spicy food, add some hot peppers too. Cook for 3 more minutes on high. To serve: Pour this over rice on a plate. Garnish with sesame seeds.

There are many different kinds of deopbap in Korea. Deopbap is basically a type of food that is served on top of rice. It is made with some food, usually meat, veggies, and/or a sauce. It is all mixed together before eating. This type has a non-spicy beef topping. The beef has bulgogi flavor, and there are many different kinds of veggies in this dish. Tip: If you have leftover marinated bulgogi, or frozen bulgogi, you can use that instead of this meat.

Chicken & Veggie Bokkeumbap

Yield: 3 Sevings

닭 야채볶음밥, Dak YaChaeBokkEumBap

INGREDIENTS

2 Cups Short Grain Rice, Cooked	Vegetable Oil for Frying
2 Eggs, Beaten	
$1/2$ Cup Onion, Finely Chopped	**For the Chicken**
$1/2$ Cup Zucchini, Finely Chopped	1 Cup Chicken Breast, $1/4$-Inch Pieces
$1/4$ Cup Carrot, Finely Chopped	$1/2$ Tbsp Cooking Wine (or Water)
$1/4$ Cup Green Onion, Finely Chopped	$1/8$ tsp Salt
3 Tbsp Celery, Finely Chopped	$1/8$ tsp Black Pepper
2 Tbsp Red Sweet Pepper, Finely Chopped	
$1/2$ Tbsp Garlic, Finely Chopped	
$1/2$ tsp Salt	
1 tsp Sesame Seeds	

For better flavor, marinate the chicken ingredients while you are preparing the other ingredients.

In a heated pan, fry the marinated chicken until it doesn't have anymore pink color.

Add all the veggies and 1 Tbsp of oil. Fry it for about 5 minutes on medium-high.

Add the rice. Fry for another 5 minutes. If needed, you can add a little more oil. In this step, add $1/2$ tsp of salt. You may want to adjust the amount of salt.

Add 2 pinches of salt to the eggs. Push the rice to one side of the pan to make space to cook the eggs. Add some more oil. Make scrambled eggs. Fry 3 more minutes on high.

Mix it and turn off the heat. You may want to add a little sesame oil. I garnished the food with sesame seeds and crown daisy leaves.

This is a delicious and nutritious dish because it has chicken, various veggies, eggs, and rice. Since you get different flavors from the ingredients, you don't need side dishes to eat with it; just kimchi and a Korean soup will give you a simple, yet perfect, meal. It matches well with many other foods, so you can serve this as a side to a meal from your own country too.

Tuna Kimchi Triangle Kimbap

참치김치 삼각김밥, ChamChiGimChi SamGakGimBap   Yield: 5 Servings

INGREDIENTS

5	Sheets Dried Laver (From Kit)
$^1/_2$	Cup Tuna in Oil, Drained
$^1/_2$	Cup Kimchi, Well Fermented, Finely Chopped
1	Tbsp Vegetable Oil
2	tsp Hot Pepper Powder
$^1/_4$	tsp Sugar

For the Rice

$2^1/_2$	Cups Short Grain Rice, Cooked
$^1/_8$	tsp Salt
1	tsp Sesame Oil
1	tsp Sesame Seeds

Combine and gently mix the rice ingredients.

Combine the tuna, kimchi, vegetable oil, hot pepper powder, and sugar in a pan. Fry for about 5 minutes on medium-high. Add more hot pepper powder or hot pepper paste to make it spicier.

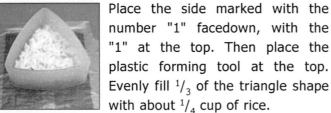
Place the side marked with the number "1" facedown, with the "1" at the top. Then place the plastic forming tool at the top. Evenly fill $^1/_3$ of the triangle shape with about $^1/_4$ cup of rice.

Add some of the filling on top of the rice. Leave about $^1/_8$-inch all around the filling; do not let the filling touch the forming tool. This helps prevent a mess later when we press it.

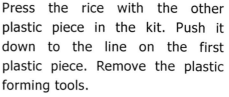
Getting the right amount of rice and filling is the key to getting the perfect taste and shape. Add another $^1/_4$ cup of rice on top of the filling.

Press the rice with the other plastic piece in the kit. Push it down to the line on the first plastic piece. Remove the plastic forming tools.

Fold the seaweed sheet up over the rice. Fold both sides of the seaweed down over the rice, and tuck the extra seaweed under the rice.

Fold both sides of the bottom seaweed piece up over the sides to the center of the triangle. Fasten each side with a piece of the tape.

For people who are too busy to prepare breakfast or lunch, this is a good option. There are many different types available; this one uses tuna and kimchi. If you have kids, it will be fun to make this together with your children.

Buckwheat Guksu

Yield: 2 Servings

메밀국수, MeMilGukSu

INGREDIENTS

1	Handful Buckwheat Noodles (and 6 Cups Water, $1/2$ tsp Salt)
2	Eggs, Beaten
2	Green Onions, $1/2$-Inch Pieces
2	Sheets Seaweed

For the Broth

4	Cups Water
5	Tbsp Guksijangguk (A Korean Soup Base)
$1^{1}/_{2}$	tsp Japanese Hondashi
$1/_{2}$	tsp Salt

Boil the noodles in 6 cups of water with $1/2$ tsp of salt for 5 minutes.

Slice the cooked flat eggs thinly and cut the toasted seaweed sheets with scissors.

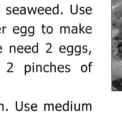

While the noodles are boiling, make the broth. In a pan, add all the ingredients for the broth.

Drain and then rinse the noodles in cold water once. Set them aside.

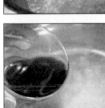

We need 2 toppings for this soup: a flat egg and dried seaweed. Use one pinch of salt per egg to make a flat egg. Since we need 2 eggs, we will be adding 2 pinches of salt.

With the broth boiling, add the noodles, and cook for 2 minutes. Then add the green onions, and cook for one more minute. Mix the egg and seaweed with the soup just before eating.

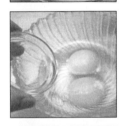

Fry the egg in a pan. Use medium heat and a little oil. Once the surface is almost done cooking, flip it. (Place the spatula in the center of the egg to help prevent the egg from breaking.)

Buckwheat is thought to be a very healthy food to eat. This is a delicious way to eat buckwheat. Buckwheat was used in making noodles before wheat. Buckwheat is thought to be good for cholesterol and blood pressure control. The nutty and slightly bitter flavors from the buckwheat noodles combination nicely with the other ingredients to make a very delicious soup.

Pine Nut Juk

잣죽, JatJuk   Yield: 3 Servings

INGREDIENTS

$^2/_3$ Cup Short Grain Rice
$^1/_2$ Cup Pine Nuts, Removed Top Part
$4^1/_2$ Cups Water
1   tsp Sugar
$^3/_4$ tsp Salt
      Some Pine Nuts (Garnish)

Wash and then soak the rice in water for about 2 hours, or at least 30 minutes if you are short on time. After the soak, drain the water. You will get about 1 cup of soaked rice.

Grind the rice with 1 cup of water in a blender until there are no chunks. I ground it for about a minute on high speed.

Strain the rice mixture to make a soft and creamy porridge. Then add 3 cups of water into the pan.

Grind the pine nuts with $^1/_2$ cup of water in a blender for about half a minute on high speed.

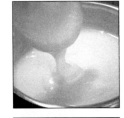

Cook for 10 to 15 minutes on medium. Keep stirring it with a wooden spoon, or it will get lumpy. When it becomes thick and starts to bubble, it is ready for the pine nuts.

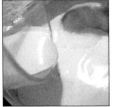

Pour the pine nut mixture into it, stirring gently. Do not to stir too much though, or the pine nuts will make it become too watery. Once it starts to boil again, cook for 3 more minutes on medium-high.

This recipe does not make thick porridge. If you want a thicker texture, you can reduce the amount of water.

After it is done cooking, add the sugar and salt. Mix gently and serve. You may want to adjust the amount of sugar and salt. You can garnish with whole or ground pine nuts.

Pine nut juk is a simple Korean porridge that is thought to be healthy. It is creamy, and it has a very good nutty flavor. This porridge is good for people who cannot chew or digest food well. It is also good for somebody that does not have much of an appetite.

Red Bean Juk

Yield: 2 Servings

팥죽, PatJuk

INGREDIENTS

2 Cups Red Bean Paste	½ Cup Water
1 Cup Water	¼ tsp Salt
2 Tbsp Sugar	
	For the Thickener
For the Rice Balls	1 Tbsp Sweet Rice Flour
²/₃ Cup Sweet Rice Flour	3 Tbsp Water
⅓ Cup Short Grain Rice Flour	

Mix and stir together the red bean paste and 1 cup of water in a pot. Ensure that the red bean paste dissolves in the water. Boil it on medium-high.

Combine and mix all the ingredients for the rice balls.

Knead the dough for several minutes to get a nice doughy texture.

Take about 1 tsp of dough and make a small ball. You will get about 40 sticky rice balls.

Once the red bean paste starts to boil, add the rice balls.

Mix together the ingredients for the thickener. Drizzle that mixture into the porridge slowly. It will help thicken the porridge. Cook the porridge for 10 to 12 minutes on medium-high.

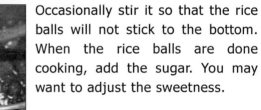

Occasionally stir it so that the rice balls will not stick to the bottom. When the rice balls are done cooking, add the sugar. You may want to adjust the sweetness.

Cook one more minute and then turn off the heat.

Red bean porridge is commonly eaten on the shortest day of the year in Korea. This warm and sweet porridge is a great meal for any winter day too. It is an easy recipe to make. The sweet and nutty flavors from the red bean paste, along with the chewy rice balls, taste great together.

Black Bean Paste Myeon

자장면, JaJangMyeon   Yield: 2 Servings

INGREDIENTS

1	Cup Onion, $1/_2$-Inch Cubes	
1	Cup Potato, $1/_2$-Inch Cubes	
$1/_2$	Cup Zucchini, $1/_2$-Inch Cubes	
2	Handful Cabbage, $1/_2$-Inch Cubes	
	Thick Noodles for JaJangMyeon	

For the Meat

$1/_2$	lb (1 Cup) Beef or Pork, $1/_2$-Inch Cubes
1	Tbsp Cooking Wine (or Water)
1	Pinch Salt
1	Pinch Black Pepper

For the Sauce

4	Tbsp Black Bean Paste
1	Tbsp Vegetable Oil
$1/_2$	tsp Sugar
2	Cups Water
2	Tbsp Cornstarch

Combine and mix all the meat ingredients. Set it aside while you are preparing other ingredients. After that, fry the meat until it has completely cooked.

In an oiled and heated pan, fry the potato until it is half done. Then, add the onion and cabbage. Fry until they are half done. Lastly, add the zucchini and fry until it all has finished cooking.

To make the sauce, start with 1 Tbsp of oil in a heated pan. Add the black bean paste and fry until it becomes soft. Add the sugar. Sugar helps to remove the bitterness of the black bean paste.

After all the veggies are cooked, add the meat and the fried black bean paste. Mix everything together.

Thoroughly mix together the ingredients for the thickener. Pour the thickener into the pan.

Boil until the sauce becomes thicker. Serve the black bean paste sauce over cooked rice or noodles. Garnish with cucumber or peas. Cucumbers taste especially good with this.

In Korea, this is the most popular Korean-Chinese food. It is a little different from what you might find served in China. The sauce is made of black bean paste, meat, and different veggies. Restaurants will deliver this to your home for around 4 dollars with no tipping. Usually this is served with yellow pickled radish (danmuji), radish kimchi (kkakdugi), black bean paste, and raw onion. Dip the onion into the black bean paste when you eat it.

Soybean Curd Chobap

Yield: 16 Pieces

유부초밥, YuBuChoBap

INGREDIENTS

1	Pack Seasoned Soybean Curd (Including Sauce)
2	Cups Short Grain Rice, Cooked
2	Tbsp Onion, Finely Chopped
1	Tbsp Carrot, Finely Chopped
1½	Tbsp Green Sweet Pepper, Finely Chopped
1½	Tbsp Red Sweet Pepper, Finely Chopped

1½ Tbsp Yellow Sweet Pepper, Finely Chopped
Some Salt

Fry the onion and carrot on high without oil in a nonstick pan.

When the onion and carrot are almost cooked, add the sweet peppers and fry for about 30 seconds more.

Add some salt to taste. These veggies are ready to mix into the rice.

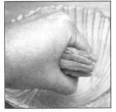
Squeeze the liquid out of the seasoned soybean curd. This package is already prepared, so simply use the soybean curd without cooking it.

In a large bowl, add the rice and the sauce from the pack. You can make your own sauce if you only buy the soybean curd, but my package already had the sauce for the rice in it.
Add the dried veggie pack and stir gently.

Add the fried veggies into the rice and mix. This makes the rice very colorful, and gives it better flavor.

Open the soybean curd as pictured. It looks like pita bread. Firmly pack the rice into the curd. You can serve this with pickled ginger, onion, or garlic.

This is a very simple yet delicious food to make. Because of that, this is very popular for picnics or parties in Korea. The rice has a sweet and sour taste. This recipe uses a ready-made package for convenience. You can add chopped burdock root, or any other kinds of veggies.

Cinnamon Cha

수정과, SuJeongGwa

Yield: 9 Cups

INGREDIENTS

10   Cups Water
12   Cinnamon Sticks or $1^3/_4$ oz, Washed
$1/_2$ Cup Ginger or $1^3/_4$ oz, Sliced
$1/_2$ Cup Sugar
$1/_2$ Cup Dark Brown Sugar
      Dried Persimmons (Optional)
      Pine Nuts (Garnish)

AERI'S TIPS

- To Reduce the strength of the cinnamon and ginger flavor, you can cut the amount, but just make sure it is a 1:1 ratio.
- Use all white sugar if you want a different color and taste.

Add 5 cups of water and the cinnamon sticks in a pan. Boil the cinnamon sticks and ginger separately on medium-high.

Add the refined sugar and dark brown sugar to the tea. Boil for 5 more minutes, or until the sugar dissolves.

In another pan, add the other 5 cups of water and the ginger. Once they start to boil, reduce the temperature to medium-low, and boil for about 30 minutes. Keep them covered.

Remove the stems of the dried persimmons. If you do not have any persimmons, you can skip them.

Discard the cinnamon sticks and ginger. Make sure you get rid of the small pieces to make the tea clear. If you have a coffee filter, use it.

Remove the tops of the pine nuts. To soften the persimmon, put it in each person's cup for an hour before they drink it. Drop some pine nuts on top just before serving.

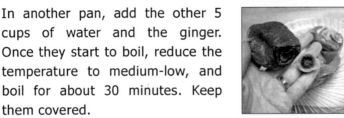

This is a traditional Korean drink made with cinnamon sticks, ginger, and sugar. Koreans usually drink this as a dessert, especially during the holidays. It tastes good both hot or cold, but I prefer it cold, with ice cubes. Once you make it, you can keep it in the fridge quite a long time.

Brown Sugar & Cinnamon Hotteok

Yield: 16 Pieces

호떡, HoTteok

$^1/_2$ Cup Warm Water
$^1/_2$ Tbsp Yeast
$^1/_2$ Tbsp Sugar
3   Cups All-Purpose Flour
1   Cup Milk
$^1/_2$ Tbsp Salt

For the Filling
$^1/_4$ Cup Brown Sugar
$^1/_4$ Cup Sugar
$1^1/_2$ Tbsp Peanuts (About 15 Peanuts), Chopped
$^1/_2$ tsp Cinnamon

Add the yeast and sugar to the warm water. Set it in warm place for 5 minutes. Meanwhile, sift the flour in a large bowl. Then add the yeast mixture, milk, and salt into the bowl.

Knead the dough. Because the dough is sticky, add flour to your hands. Form the dough into a ball and cover it with plastic wrap. Set the dough in the oven with just the light on for 3 hours.

Combine and mix the filling ingredients. To crush the peanuts: place them inside of a zipper bag and crush them with something like the back of a knife.

After 3 hours, the dough will double in size. Oil your hands before working with the dough.

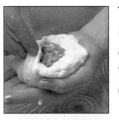

Take a piece of dough a little larger than a golf ball. Then roll and flatten it. Add a spoonful of the filling to the center. Wrap the dough around the filling.

Form it into a round ball. Shape and smooth all the creases in the dough.

Pour some oil into a preheated pan on medium-high. Place the dough balls into the pan.

About 10 seconds later, flip them over and flatten them with a spatula. Fry until both sides become golden brown.

Hotteok is a "traditional" Korean street vendor food. Korean people love to eat this delicious snack, especially in the cold winter. It tastes best when it is warm. You can easily find the ingredients for this recipe anywhere. Do you like sticky buns or pecan rolls? If so, you will love these.

Green Tea Ice Cream

녹차 아이스크림, NokCha AISeuKeuRim

Yield: 1 Quart

INGREDIENTS

2	tsp Green Tea Powder
1	Container (1 Pint) Half and Half
4	Egg Yolks
$\frac{1}{2}$	Cup Sugar

AERI'S TIPS

- Cooking the egg yolks just makes them safe to eat. You do not want to cook them too much. Make sure you keep the temperature low.
- Mixing the green tea powder with the sugar helps the powder to more evenly disperse in the ice cream mixture later.

Mix the 4 egg yolks and about $\frac{1}{4}$ cup of the half and half in a bowl. Boil the egg mixture for about 10 minutes on low in a nonstick pan. Occasionally stir it.

Mix the green tea powder and sugar together. Add the green tea mixture to the eggs. Stir until the sugar dissolves.

Mix in the remaining half and half and pour it into a container for freezing. It is good to use a wide-bottomed bowl with a lid. Put it in the freezer for about 3 hours.

After the 3 hours are up, mix the ice cream. Press it back down flat before you put it back into the freezer.

Every hour, repeat this process for at least 4 more times. This process will make your ice cream softer. Depending on your green tea powder, the color and taste can be slightly different.

In Korea, there are many popular foods made or flavored with green tea. This green tea ice cream is one of them. This recipe is especially for people who do not have an ice cream machine like me. It will be icier than store bought ice cream, but I actually prefer that kind of texture for my ice cream. If you have an ice cream machine, you can use it too.

Cake Crumb Gyeongdan

Yield: 1 Dozen Cakes

경단, GyeongDan

INGREDIENTS

$1/3$	Cup Walnuts, $1/4$-Inch Pieces		1	Cup Water
$1/2$	Yellow Cake (13 x 9 Inch Pan), Crumbs (Remove Brown Edge)		2	Tbsp Sugar
$1/3$	Cup Honey		$1/2$	tsp Salt

For the Rice
1   Cup Sweet Rice Flour

Mix together the dry ingredients for the rice, and then mix in the water. Depending on your tastes, you can skip the sugar. Stir it well enough to make a batter.

Cover it with plastic wrap. Cook it in the microwave for 3 to 6 minutes. It took my microwave 3 minutes at full power. According to the power of your microwave, it may take longer or shorter.

When the batter becomes very elastic, it is done. Knead the dough with a fork for at least 5 minutes.

Add the chopped walnuts to the dough. Mix gently so that the walnut pieces will not become too small.

In a small bowl, mix 1 cup of water and 1 pinch of salt. The salt water will help you work with the sticky rice cakes. Get some water on your hands before you touch the sticky rice dough.

Take a small ball of sticky rice cake dough, and make it into the shape of a ball.

Roll the rice cake ball on the honey.

Then roll it in the cake crumbs. This will not taste good the next day, so I recommend that you eat this right after you make it.

Gyeongdan is a traditional Korean dessert. Traditionally, you would cover the sticky rice cakes with mung bean crumbs, black sesame seeds, soybean powder, etc. However, this modern version uses cake crumbs with honey and walnuts. Since the honey and cake crumbs are sweet, you may not need sugar in the batter. On the other hand, if you like sweet food, you can add 2 Tbsp of sugar in the batter.

Red Bean Bingsu

팥빙수, PatBingSu

Yield: 1 Serving

INGREDIENTS

1¹/₂ Cups Crushed Ice
¹/₈ Cup Milk
3 Tbsp Red Beans for PotBingSu
2 Tbsp Condensed Milk
2 Tbsp Crushed Pineapple
3 Tbsp Watermelon, Finely Diced
2 Tbsp Sticky Rice Cakes for PotBingSu
2 Tbsp Corn Flakes

 Grind some ice to get 1¹/₂ cups of crushed ice.

 Place the pineapple and watermelon on top.

 In a serving bowl or cup, add the crushed ice and milk. Put the red beans on top of the ice.

 Add the sticky rice cakes and corn flakes on top of everything. It looks very colorful and cool. Before eating, mix everything together.

 Add the condensed milk on top of the red beans. This amount controls the sweetness.

Red bean bingsu is a summer dessert that many people requested. I was amazed to see how many people knew about this Korean dessert and loved it. All the ingredients combine to give you a surprisingly good flavor. Of course, it is a very cool dessert for the hot summer days. This recipe will give you an authentic taste for this dessert, but you can adjust the recipe depending on your tastes or preferences.

Korean Twisted Donuts

Yield: 2 Dozen Donuts

꽈배기 도너츠, KkwaBaeGi DoNeoCheu

INGREDIENTS

3 Cups All-Purpose Flour	Sugar for Coating
1 Cup Lukewarm Water	Vegetable Oil for Deep Frying
1 Egg	
4 Tbsp Sugar	
5 Tbsp Butter	
1$\frac{1}{2}$ Tbsp Yeast	
1 tsp Salt	

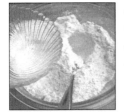 Add the flour, 4 Tbsp of sugar, butter, yeast, and salt. Quickly mix everything together. Then, mix in the egg and the lukewarm water.

 Knead the dough for least 15 minutes until it becomes elastic.

 Form the dough into a ball. Cover it with plastic wrap. Let it rise for about 1 hour in a slightly warm place until the dough size doubles. If it is at room temperature, it will take more than an hour.

Divide the dough into about 24 pieces. You can start by dividing the dough into 4 pieces. Then divide each of those pieces into 4 to 6 smaller pieces. Round each piece to make a ball.

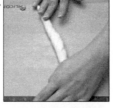 Roll a ball of the dough out to about a 12-inch length. While you are rolling it, twist each end in the opposite direction so that the dough will become twisted when you release the tension.

 Let the dough wrap around itself to form the twisted shape. Set it aside for about 10 minutes to rise again.

 Fry the donuts. When one side becomes golden brown, flip it over. Only flip it over once. If you flip it often, then the doughnut will become too greasy.

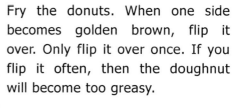 After frying the donuts, cool them for about 5 minutes. Then, in a plastic bag, add some sugar and a couple of the cooled donuts. Shake them.

In Korea, you can get these tasty donuts from a street vendor or a bakery. These donuts are delicious and fun to make with ingredients that you usually have at home. These donuts are best to eat shortly after cooking. If you want to eat some later (like the next day), freeze them in a plastic bag. Heat the frozen donuts in the microwave for a couple seconds right before eating. They will taste just as great as freshly made donuts.

Date & Ginger Cha

대추 생강차, DaeChu SaengGangCha

Yield: 4 Cups

20	Dried Dates (10 oz), Washed and Drained
1/4	Cup Ginger, Sliced
6	Cups Water
1/2	Cup Honey
	Some Dates and Pine Nuts (Garnish)

Boil the ginger and dates in the water for 20 minutes on medium-high.

Remove the tops of the pine nuts.

Prepare the date garnish. Remove the seeds by cutting the fruit and the skin away from the seeds without breaking the flesh. Roll up the date flesh and slice it. It should have a flower shape.

Add the honey and cook for 5 more minutes on high. You may want to adjust the amount of sweetness with sugar or honey.

Drain the tea and discard the dates and ginger. Garnish the tea with pine nuts and a slice of a date before serving.

Date and ginger cha is a simple homemade tea. It is good either hot or cold. It tastes good and it is thought to be good for colds. Many Koreans believe that dates and ginger help keep the body warm, so it is especially good in the winter. Dates, ginger, honey, and pine nuts are all thought to be healthy ingredients too.

Sweet Potato Mattang

Yield: 3 Servings

고구마 맛탕, GoGuMa MatTang

INGREDIENTS

3   Cups Sweet Potatoes, Peeled and Cubed
6   Tbsp Sugar or Brown Sugar
6   Tbsp Corn Syrup or Honey
1¹/₂ Tbsp Oil (Canola or Vegetable)
     Some Black Sesame Seeds or Sesame Seeds
     (Garnish)
     Vegetable Oil For Deep Frying

Soak the chopped sweet potatoes in water for 10 minutes to leech out some of the starch. That will make them more crispy and sweeter when you fry them.

Dry them with a paper towel so that you will not get hurt when you fry them. Preheat the oil to about 340°F.

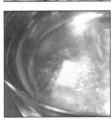

Drop in a piece of sweet potato. If it starts to boil in the oil, the oil is hot enough. Fry the sweet potatoes, occasionally stirring them so that they do not stick to the pan or each other.

To see if the potatoes are done, poke one piece with a fork or chopstick. If it goes through smoothly, they are done.

Remove them from the oil, and let any excess oil soak into a few paper towels while they are waiting for the syrup.

Boil the sugar, corn syrup, and vegetable oil on medium low until the sugar melts. It is important not to cook on high (too quickly) or the sauce will harden like candy when it cools.

Pour the hot syrup quickly on the fried sweet potatoes. Quickly mix them gently.

You can sprinkle some black or regular sesame seeds on top for decoration and extra flavor.

This is a dessert made with sweet potatoes. It tastes best when it is still warm, right after making it. Korean sweet potatoes are different from American sweet potatoes in taste, texture, and color. They are more sweet and drier. This can be a snack food for kids.

Sweet Rice & Red Bean Tteok

찹쌀떡, ChapSsalTteok   Yield: 8 Pieces

INGREDIENTS

1	Cup Sweet Rice Flour
$^1/_2$	tsp Salt
$3^1/_2$	Tbsp Sugar
1	Cup Water
$^3/_4$	Cup Red Bean Paste
	Some Cornstarch

Mix the sweet rice flour, sugar, and salt. Slowly mix in the water. Stir it until all the ingredients are blended.

Cover it with plastic wrap. Cook it in the microwave for 3 minutes, take it out, and stir it. (Depending on your microwave's power, you may have to adjust the time. Mine took 3 minutes on high.)

If the dough is very elastic, it is done. (Please check my video on YouTube for a better visual.) Stir the dough for at least 3 minutes.

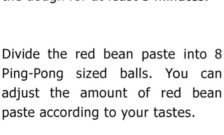

Divide the red bean paste into 8 Ping-Pong sized balls. You can adjust the amount of red bean paste according to your tastes.

Sprinkle a little cornstarch on a cutting board. Roll the dough into a 16-inch long loaf.

Cut the dough into eight 2-inch pieces. Flatten a piece.

Place the bean ball in the center. Wrap the ball with the rice dough.

Roll it out smooth and cover it with more cornstarch.

Korean people have been eating rice cakes for a long time. This one is mainly made with sweet rice flour and red bean paste. Cookies, pies, cakes, and candy are popular desserts in the West, whereas rice cakes and fruit are popular in Korea, although that is starting to change. So, Korean rice cakes are not eaten as much as before. However, these are still popular for special events such as holidays, birthdays, etc.

Red Bean Ice Cream

Yield: 7 Servings

팥 아이스크림, Pat AISeuKeuRim

INGREDIENTS

1	Cup Red Bean Paste
1	Cup Whipping Cream
$^1/_2$	Cup Milk
3	Tbsp Sugar

 Obtain the red bean paste. You can use my homemade red bean paste recipe, or you can use a can from the store.

 Combine the red bean paste, whipping cream, milk, and sugar in a mixing bowl.

 Mix everything together with a whisk. Taste it, because you might want to increase the amount of sugar. Once it hardens, it will taste a little less sweet, so consider that.

 Pour the mixture into popsicle molds.

 You will get about 7 to 8 popsicles.

 Freeze it for at least 6 hours in your freezer.

Red bean ice cream is one of the things you can make with homemade red bean paste. So if you decided to try my recipe for that, this ice cream recipe will be a good use for it. We have a very popular red bean ice cream bar called "bibibig" in Korea. It has a good red bean flavor along with a sweet milky flavor. It is harder than normal ice cream. My recipe tastes very similar to bibibig.

Dumpling Wrapper Hotteok

만두피 호떡, ManDuPi HoTteok

Yield: 8 Servings

INGREDIENTS

16	Dumpling Wrappers		1	Tbsp White Sugar
	Vegetable Oil for Frying		¹/₂	tsp Cinnamon Powder
			1	Pinch Salt

For the Filling
2   Tbsp Almonds, Crushed
2   Tbsp Pecans, Crushed
¹/₃ Cup Dark Brown Sugar

Place the sliced almonds and pecans inside of a zipper bag. Chop them with the back of a knife until they become crumbly.

Mix together the ingredients for the filling.

Spread a little bit of water around the edge of a dumpling wrapper. This step helps the wrapper to seal and stick together.

Put about 1 or 2 Tbsp of filling in the center of the wrapper.

Put some water around the inside edge of the other wrapper and put it on top of the first wrapper.

To seal them tight, press the wrappers together with a fork. The fork gives the hotteok a pretty pattern. If your dumpling wrappers are too dry or hard, they will not stick together well.

Place the hotteok in a generously oiled and heated pan.

Fry them on medium until both sides of the hotteok become golden brown.

This is a quick and delicious crispy hotteok using left over dumpling wrappers. It takes time to make the dough for traditional hotteok, and it is also a little difficult to handle that sticky dough. So, this is an easy and fast way to make hotteok. Of course, the texture will be very different, but the flavor is good enough to satisfy. You can use any kind of nuts, or even some roasted sesame seeds, but just make sure that they are unsalted and unseasoned.

Cannellini Bean Gwaja

Yield: 50 Cookies

상투과자, SangTuGwaJa

INGREDIENTS

1¹/₂ Cups White Kidney Bean Paste
¹/₂ Cup Almond Powder
1   Egg Yolk
2   Tbsp Milk

You can make your own almond powder by grinding ¹/₂ cup of sliced almonds.

Obtain the Cannellini bean paste. I used pre-made paste for this recipe. It is also used in various other Korean snacks and desserts.

Combine the bean paste, almond powder, milk, and egg yolk into a mixing bowl.

Mix everything together until you get a smooth paste with a texture like peanut butter.

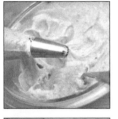

Put the bean paste mixture into a cake decorating pouch and put a ¹/₂-inch cake decorating tip on the end. Preheat the oven to 350°F. Place a piece of wax paper on top of a baking sheet.

Hold the bag at a 90° angle, about ¹/₄-inch above the wax paper, and start to squeeze. Once the cookie is about 1-inch in diameter, slowly stop squeezing while lifting up.

Bake the cookies for 20 to 25 minutes, or until the outside is slightly golden brown, and the inside is cooked.

Cannellini bean cookies can easily be found in Korean bakeries. These cookies got their name because they look like topknot haircuts, "sangtu," which was the traditional haircut for married men. This recipe has no flour in it, which makes it great for those who have an allergy to wheat. My husband said he was surprised by that when he tried them for the first time. They are slightly chewy, but mostly cake-like: as if they contain flour. They are very tasty and sweet.

Sweet Red Bean Bbang

단팥빵, DanPatBbang   Yield: 16 Servings

INGREDIENTS

$3^1/_2$ Cups All-Purpose Flour
$2^1/_2$ Cups Red Bean Paste
$^2/_3$ Cup Water, Lukewarm
$^2/_3$ Cup Milk, Lukewarm
$^1/_4$ Cup Sugar
$^1/_4$ Cup Butter, Melted
2   tsp Fast Active Dry Yeast

$1^1/_2$ tsp Salt
Some Melted Butter (for Brushing)
Some Black Sesame Seeds (to Garnish)

Place the flour in a big mixing bowl and make three holes. In the holes, place the sugar, yeast, and salt. Gently cover the holes. Add the water and milk. Mix everything with a fork or your hands.

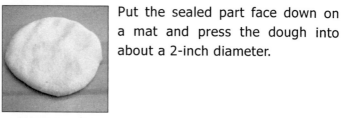

Fold the dough up and over the red bean paste to cover it. Seal the center tightly so that the red bean paste will not come out.

Add the butter. If you have a bread machine, let it do the work. If you knead the dough by hand, strongly knead for about 30 minutes, or until it becomes smooth and elastic.

Put the sealed part face down on a mat and press the dough into about a 2-inch diameter.

Loosely cover the bowl with plastic wrap and set it in a warm place for about 40 minutes. Meanwhile, divide the bean paste into 16 pieces and form them into round balls.

Cut 8 decorative slits around the edge, equally spaced apart. Put some black sesame seeds in the center. Press gently to help them stick. You can substitute regular sesame seeds or crushed nuts.

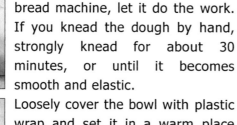

Divide the dough into 16 pieces and form them into round balls. Flatten each ball until it is about a 3-inch diameter and then place 1 red bean ball in the center.

Let them rise on a baking sheet for 15 minutes. Preheat the oven to 350°F. Bake for 20 minutes, or until golden brown. Brush the top with egg before baking them, or melted butter after baking them.

Sweet red bean bbang is an old-fashioned bakery product. There are many different kinds of sweet foods that use red bean paste. This is one of the most popular ones. If you have a bread machine, you can make this very easy dessert at home. Warm, freshly baked bread tastes very good with sweet bean filling.

Sweet Rice Eumryo

Yield: 2¹/₂ Quarts

식혜, SikHye

INGREDIENTS

2	Cups Coarse Malted Barley Powder
10	Cups Water
2	Cups Short Grain Rice, Cooked but a Little Dry
³/₄	Cup Sugar

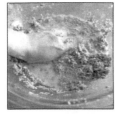

Soak the barley powder in 6 cups of cold water for an hour. The barley will become softer. Then rub and squeeze it in the water for a few minutes to make the water milky. Strain it. Save the water.

Add 4 cups of water to the leftover barley powder. Rub and squeeze it again for several minutes. Strain the milky water, and combine it with the first straining.

Leave the barley water sit for 6 hours, or overnight, in the refrigerator. The powder will sink to the bottom and clear water will be on top.

Along with the rice, fill your rice cooker almost to the top with the water from the barley mixture. Do not to let any of the powder go in. Cook it using the "keep warm" function for about 3 hours.

Pour any leftover barley water into a separate container and save it for later. Discard the leftover powder from the bottom.

When about 20 pieces of rice float, it is done. Your rice cooker's time may be different. Remove 1 cup of rice. Put it in a container with a little bit of cold water. Keep it in your refrigerator.

Pour the contents of the rice cooker, and the leftover barley water from earlier, into a pot. Boil on medium-high. Add the sugar. Occasionally skim the foam from the surface (improves the flavor).

Cook for 15 minutes and then turn off the heat. Cool the drink before serving. To serve: pour some in a bowl or cup, and then add some of the rice that you saved earlier. The rice will float on top.

This is one of the most common and popular traditional holiday drinks in Korea. There are not many ingredients in it; however, it takes long time to make it. That is why it is a special drink for holidays. It tastes a little like iced tea, but it has a unique barley and rice flavor. It is my favorite Korean drink.

Glossary

Bap: cooked rice

Bbang: bread

BibimGukSu: noodles mixed with other ingredients and sauce

BingSu: crushed ice with a syrup on top

BokkEum: pan-fried food

BokkEumBap: pan-fried rice

BokkEumTang: pan-fried food in a boiled down broth

BuChim: pan-fried food, usually covered with a batter or flour and egg

BulGoGi: barbecued beef, chicken, or pork

Cha: tea

ChoBap: cooked rice, seasoned with vinegar

ChoJeolIm: pickled food with vinegar

ChoMuChim: a type of muchim with vinegar added

DeopBap: a topping poured over cooked rice

EumRyo: a beverage

GalBi: barbecued ribs, usually short ribs

GgoChi: skewered food

Guk: soup

GukSu: noodles

GwaJa: crackers, cookies, biscuits, chips, or other similar snack foods

GyeongDan: stuffed sticky rice cake balls, usually covered with sesame seeds, cake crumbs, or other ingredients

HoTteok: stuffed pancakes, usually with cinnamon and sugar

JangTteok: a type of unsweetened pancake made with veggies or other ingredients, using a batter seasoned with soybean paste or hot pepper paste

Jeon: a type of unsweetened pancake that contains different kinds of veggies and/or meat

JjiGae: stew

Jjim: steamed or boiled, meat or seafood, usually marinated

JjimDak: chicken which has been marinated and cooked in a sauce or soup

JoRim: boiled down food in soy sauce or other seasonings

Juk: porridge

JuMeokBap: a round ball of cooked rice, the shape of a fist, to be eaten with the hands

KimBap: various ingredients rolled in white rice and dried laver

Kimchi: a traditional fermented Korean dish made with veggies and a variety of seasonings

MaeUnTang: spicy tang, usually containing fish

MatTang: deep-fried veggies or fruit covered with a sugary syrup

MuChim: seasoned fresh veggies, dried fish, or seaweed

Myeon: noodles

NaengChae: a dish that has julienned veggies or meat, served cold

NaengGuk: a soup with a clear broth, usually containing soy sauce or vinegar, served cold

NaMul: boiled veggies with some seasonings

SuJeBi: clear soup with small dough dumplings

Tang: soup, with a thicker broth than guk

TangSuYuk: battered and deep fried meat, with a sweet and sour sauce

TongDak: deep-fried battered chicken, with special sauce

Tteok: sticky rice cakes

TteokBokkI: sticky rice cakes, usually in a sweet and spicy sauce

TwiGim: deep-fried food

16999108R00061

Made in the USA
Middletown, DE
02 January 2015